SPRINGTIME IN BYZANTIUM

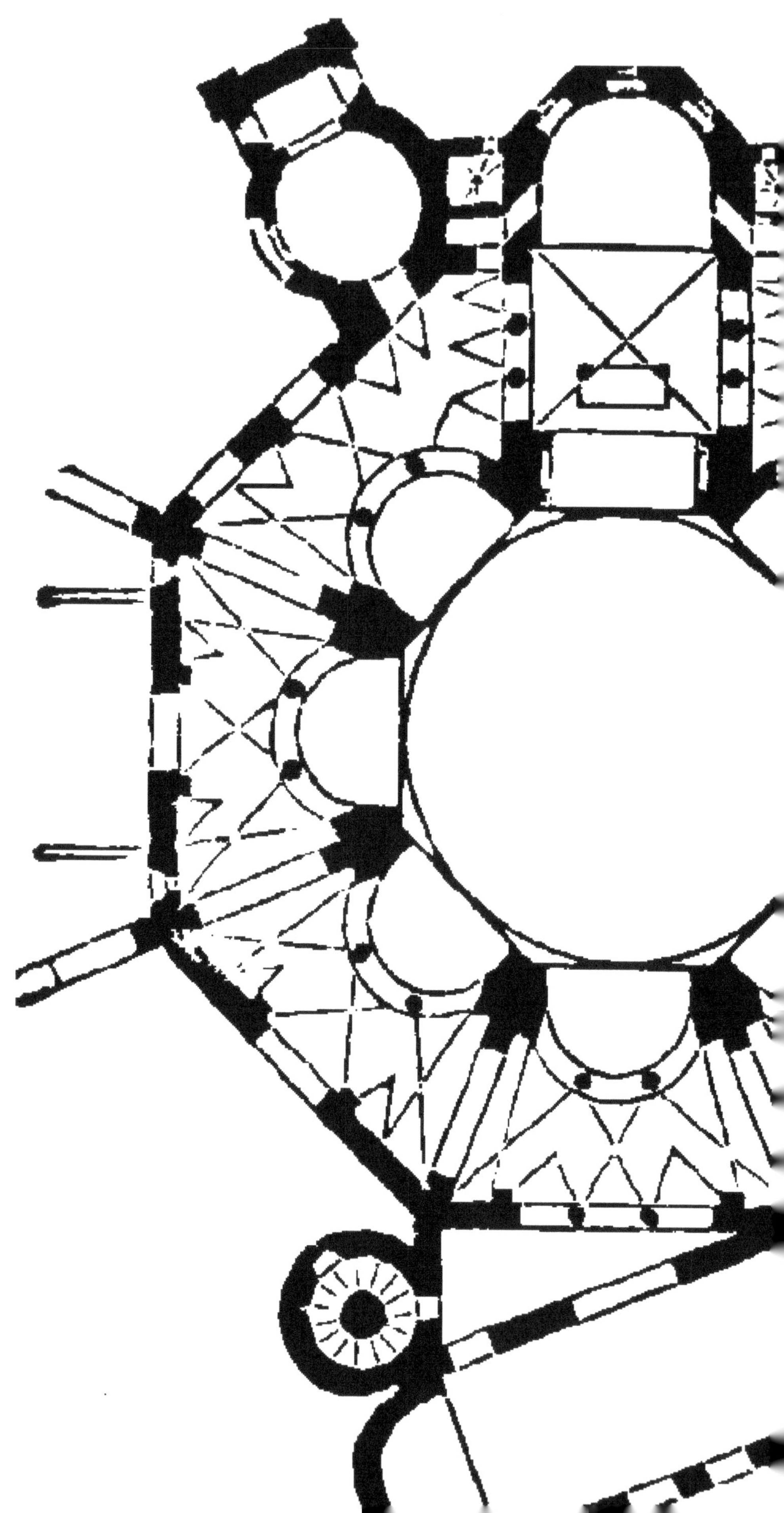

bd
nyc

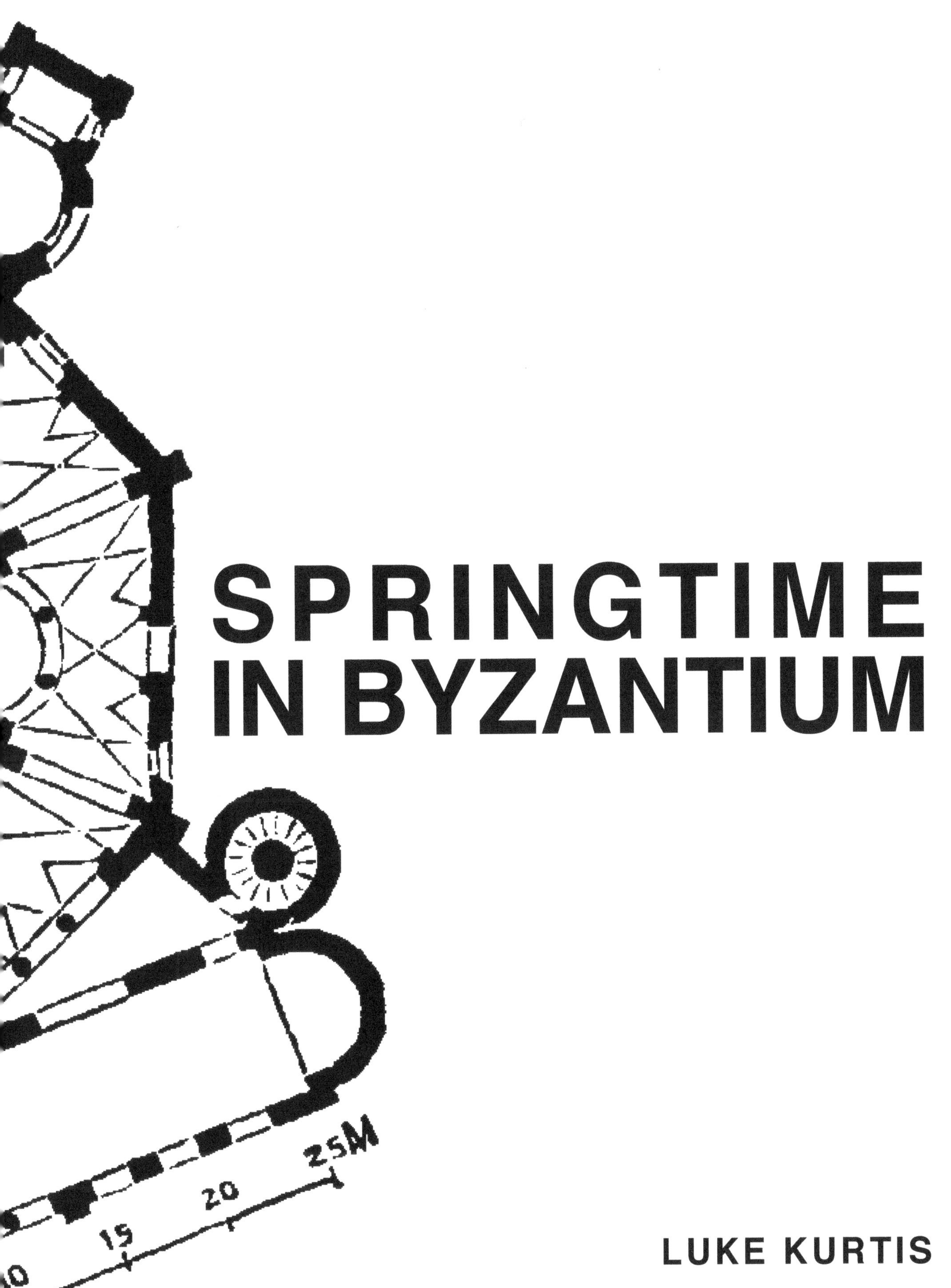

SPRINGTIME IN BYZANTIUM

LUKE KURTIS

art is for the mind

introductory text

theodora

poem

marble paintings

photographs

labyrinth

video stills

also includes photographs of San Vitale
and digital collage works

art is for the mind

Springtime in Byzantium collects three distinct but related works—*theodora*, *labyrinth*, and *marble paintings*—along with associated photographs and digital collage pieces. All are combined here in book form to create a new work structured around the Basilica of San Vitale in Ravenna, Italy.

The poem *theodora* was composed in 2011, inspired by the Basilica. Based only on my impressions from viewing photos and reading about the Byzantine architectural treasure, it's impressive just how much this text anticipated my actual experience visiting San Vitale in 2014. By the time I visited, the poem, being several years old at that point, was not consciously in my mind. Its relationship to *labyrinth* is purely coincidental (or, at least, sub-conscious).

labyrinth is a performance and video art piece I created in San Vitale. The work was conceived on the spot and without premeditation, inspired by the mosaic labyrinth found in the nave. It is related to my *journey* series of performances and video works. But where *journey* is an adaptable work that I have performed in several locations and settings, *labyrinth* is site-specific, designed specifically for the space.

I also made the *marble paintings* series of photographs in San Vitale. The marble panels that decorate the piers of the exedrae extending just off the central nave, though understated by comparison to the beautiful mosaics the church is so well known for, immediately jumped out at me for their abstract, bookmatched forms. I often employ this same kaleidoscope-like pattern in many of my works, such as the *Language Tiles* seen in *The Language of History*. Straight away, I set out to make the photos you see here.

Similar panels decorate Hagia Sophia in Istanbul, another Byzantine treasure which I visited years ago.

Writing in 564 C.E., Paul the Silentiary described those panels: "The joining of the cut marbles resembles the art of painting for you may see the veins of the square and octagonal stones meeting so as to form devices: connected in this way, the stones imitate the glories of painting."

This sensitivity to an ancient and somewhat avant-garde form reflects my own sensibilities of combining mediums or, more precisely, using one medium in the manner of another.

Though I have not undertaken an exhaustive study, I have noted bookmatched designs, such as the Basilica of Santa Maria Assunta (Torcello, Venice, Italy), which also dates to the Byzantine period. The church features lesser-known mosaics compared to those in Ravenna and bookmatched marble panels in the central apse and on the west wall. The Basilica of San Marco in Venice even features bookmatched panels. It is well known how the Venetians fashioned themselves as Byzantium's heirs in much the way the Byzantines fashioned themselves as the heirs of Rome. That is expressed in many ways through art and architecture but perhaps nowhere more subtly yet clearly than in the use of bookmatched marble at San Marco.

I'm keen to collect other examples of bookmatched marble, and I enjoy noting them when I encounter them in the wild. I was amused to see such panels as a significant element of Minoru Yamasaki's Northwestern National Life Building (1965) in Minneapolis. I even noted such a design in a Manhattan bath and kitchen tile showroom. The way this motif is equally suited to ancient and contemporary design is precisely what makes it so notable to me.

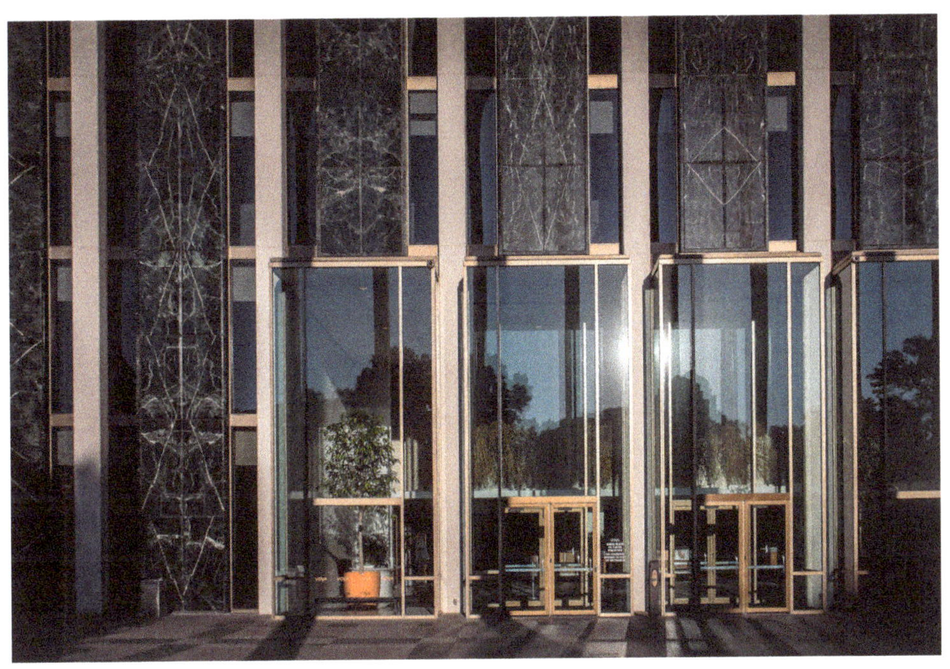

bookmatch, 2016
Minneapolis, Minnesota

Springtime in Byzantium brings together these works—poetry, photograpahy, video, performance, and digital collage—unified not in style or medium but, instead, in the execution of a common breed of ideas. This unity of thought is at the core of my practice. It is the notion of "idea" that I elevate, not the exaltation of technical skill or even aesthetic vision. All art is for the mind, and here I present to you a bit of mine.

theodora

the skin is slick with heat
the air so still
my breath is like a rush of wind

i dream of springtime in byzantium
a calm melody floats nearby
while chapels glisten with vivid mosaic

each step a calm patter
i draw out each measure
shuffling my weight about

the delicate dance
of nature awakening
is a bold meditation

the roots of plants
though unseen
are vital to photosynthesis

the soil is rich with moisture
beyond the grasp of my thirst
and unquenched desire

love travels yet higher
through ancient highways
all roads lead to rome

to desolate angels
born on crimson wing
weeping

to spring breezes
shattered with crystal memory
falling

to quiet moments
given for thoughtful prayer
calling

beyond the stars
and holy corridors
i have traveled

and here i am before your throne
kneeling at your feet
a servant bid farewell

this awareness
this eternal mind
is everywhere

i am that
i am nothing
i am everything

though the body may be frail
i seek a calm place
of silent refuge

i seek a place for all seasons
where i may live out my days
calling to you

and waiting for an answer

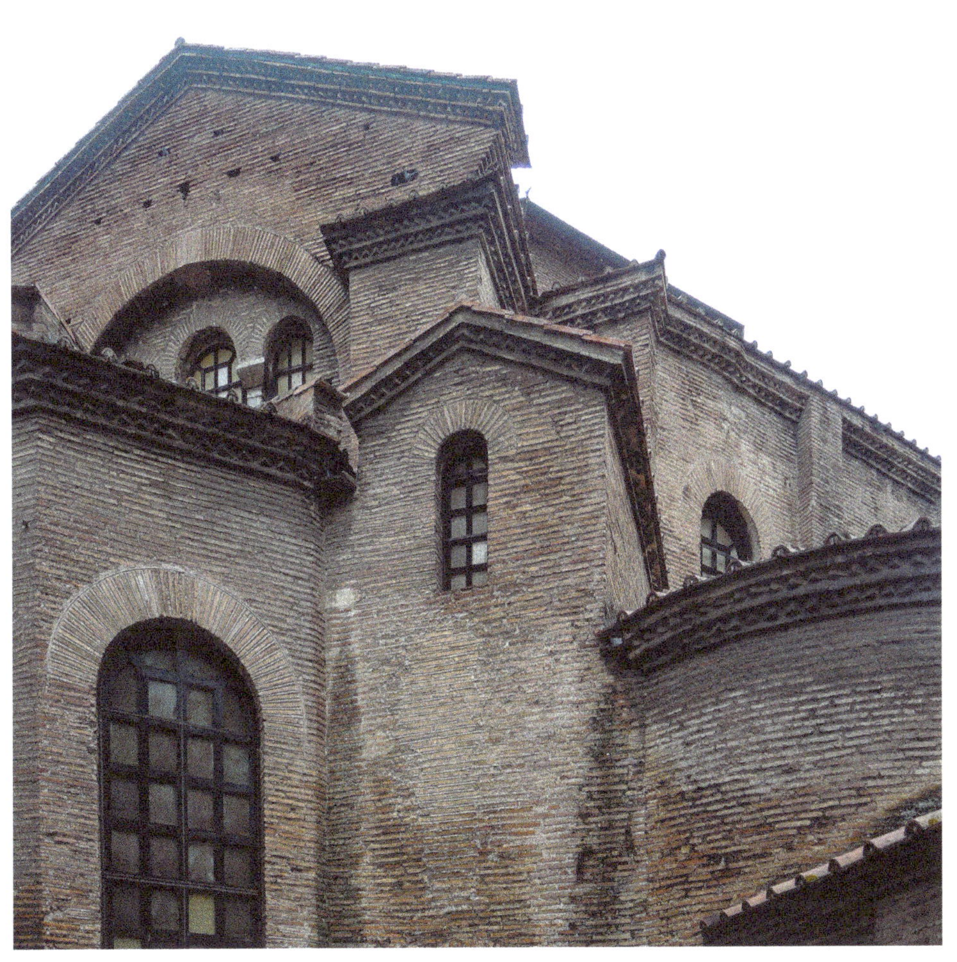

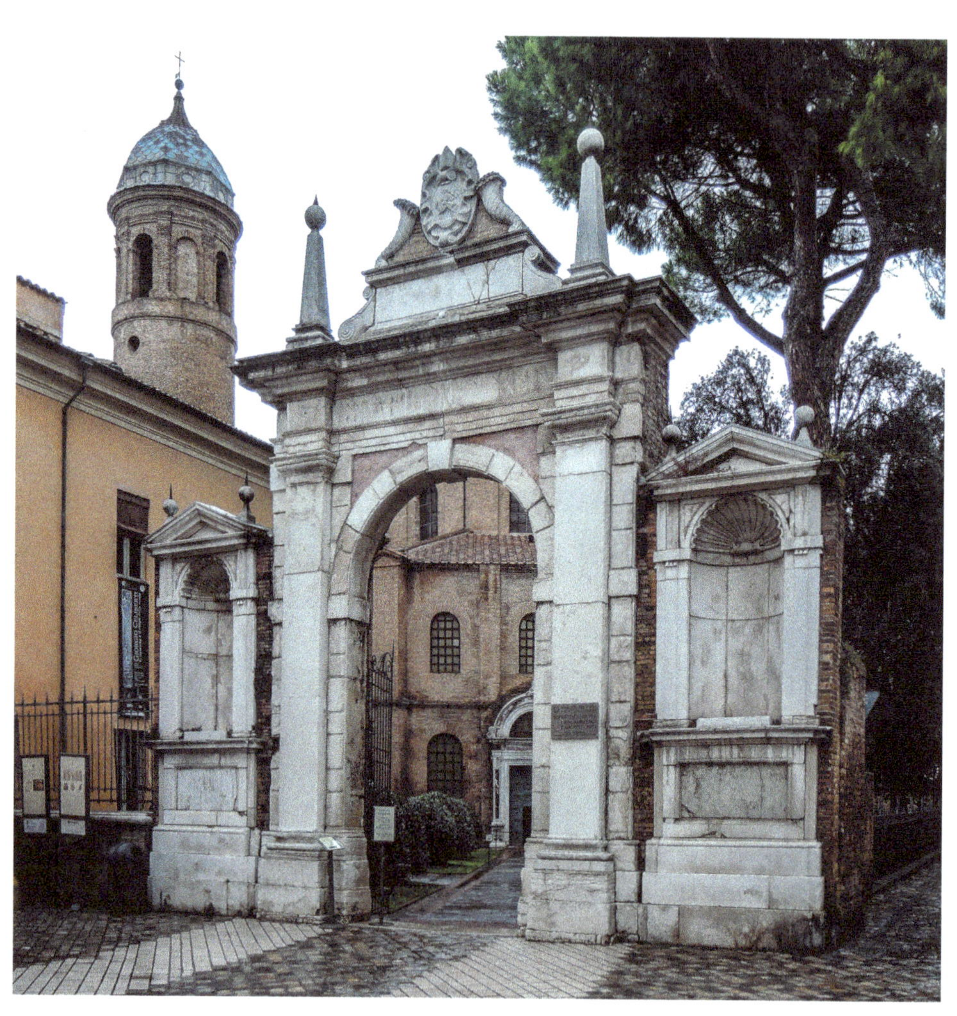

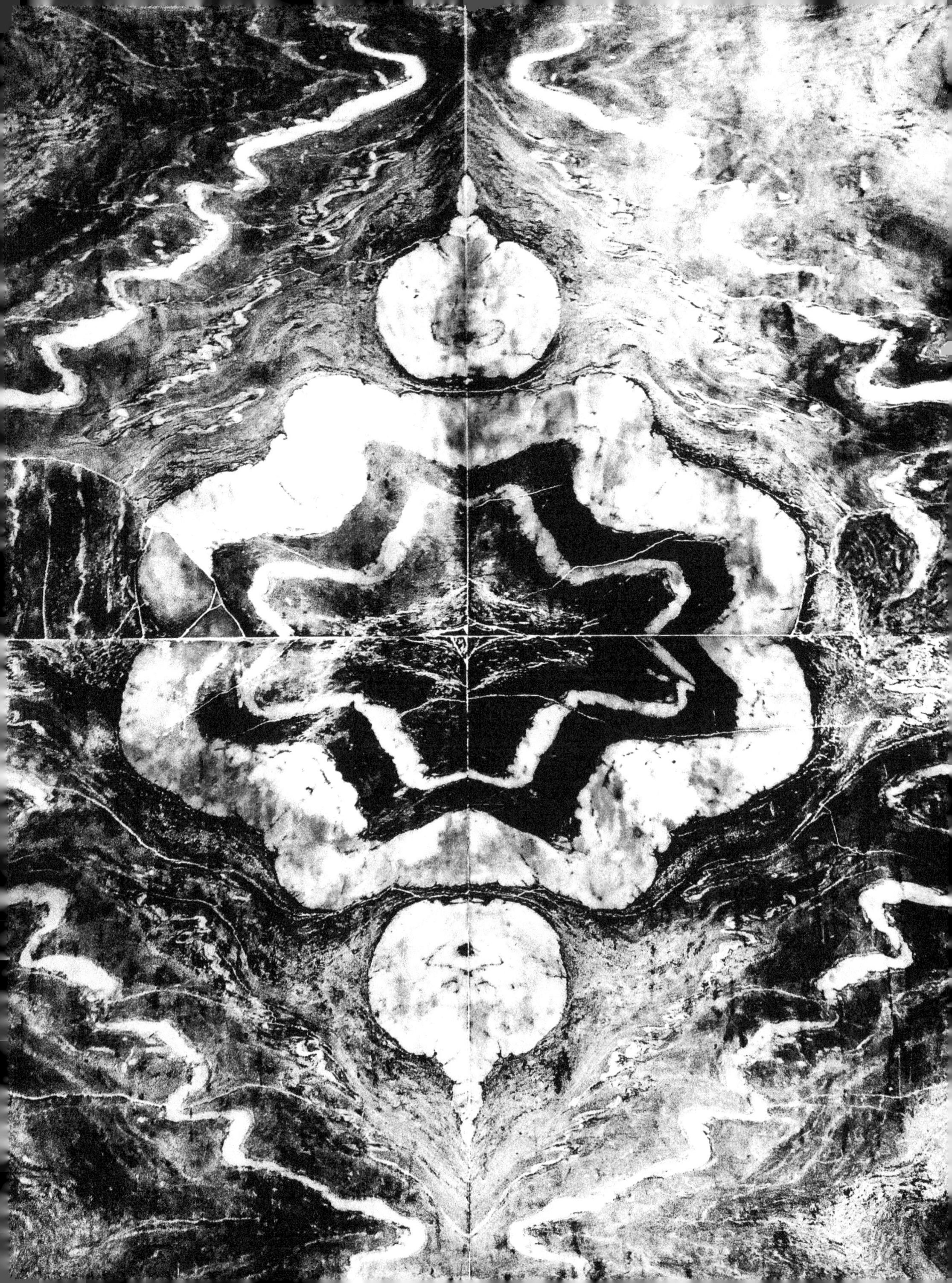

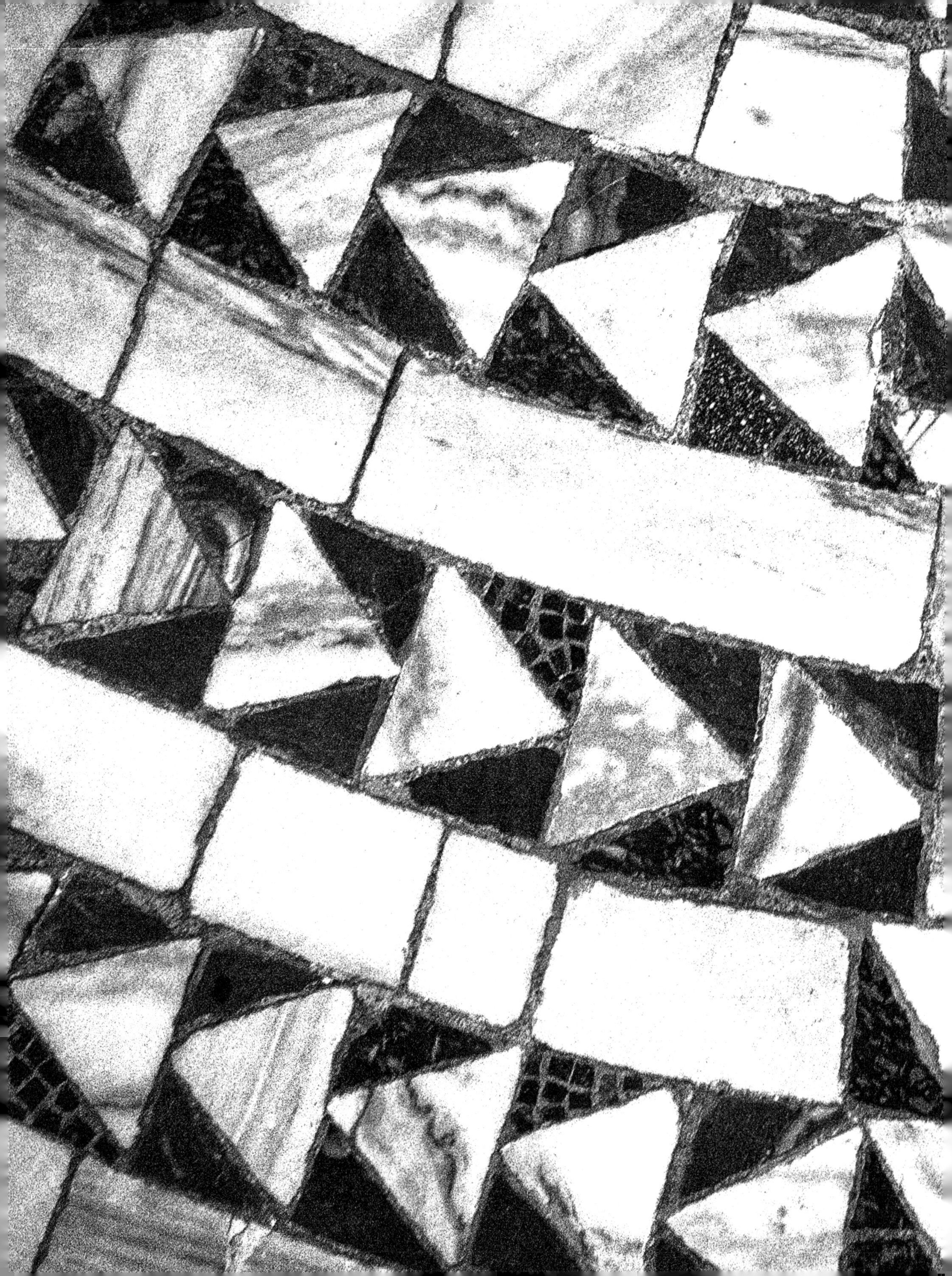

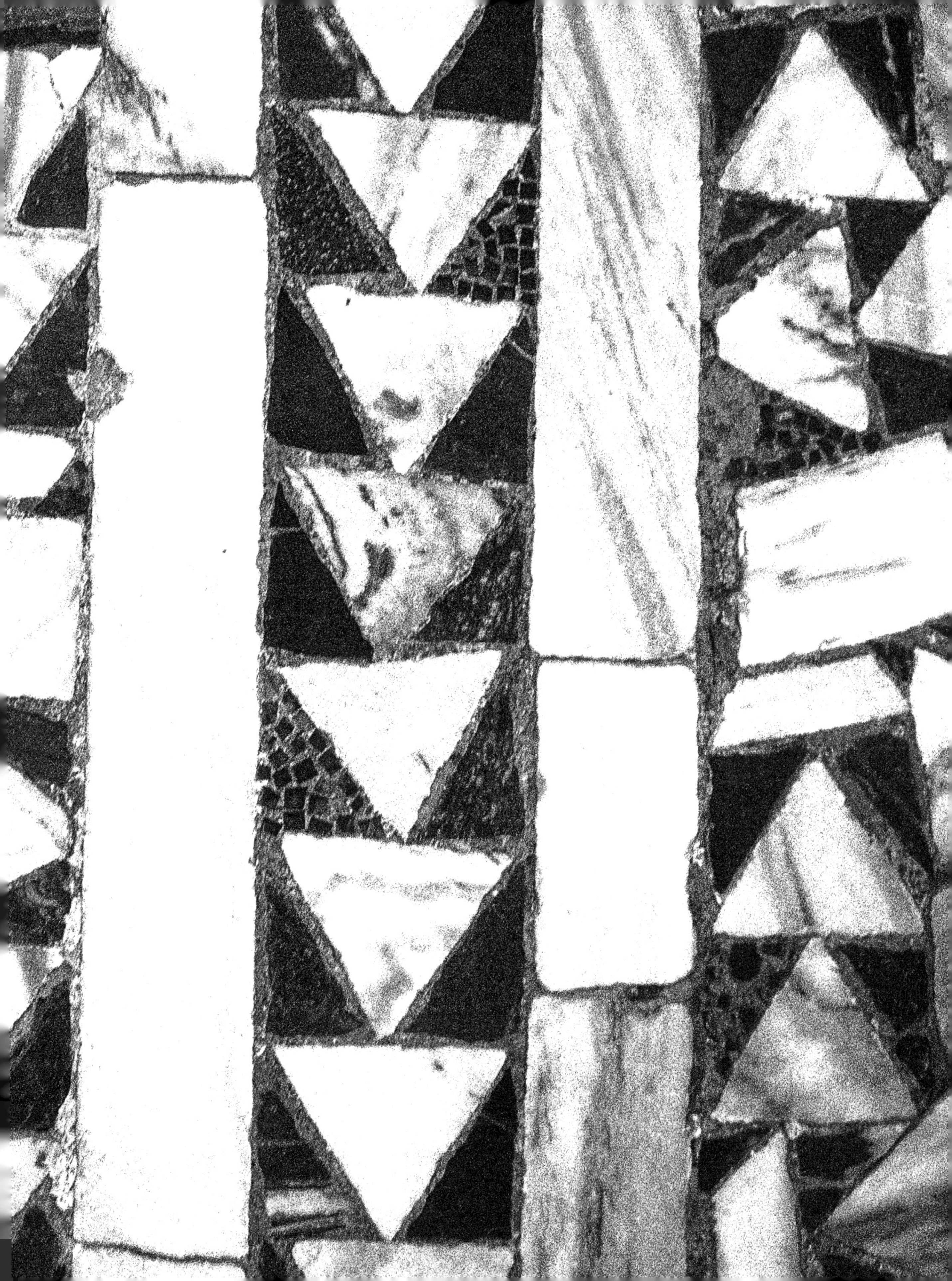

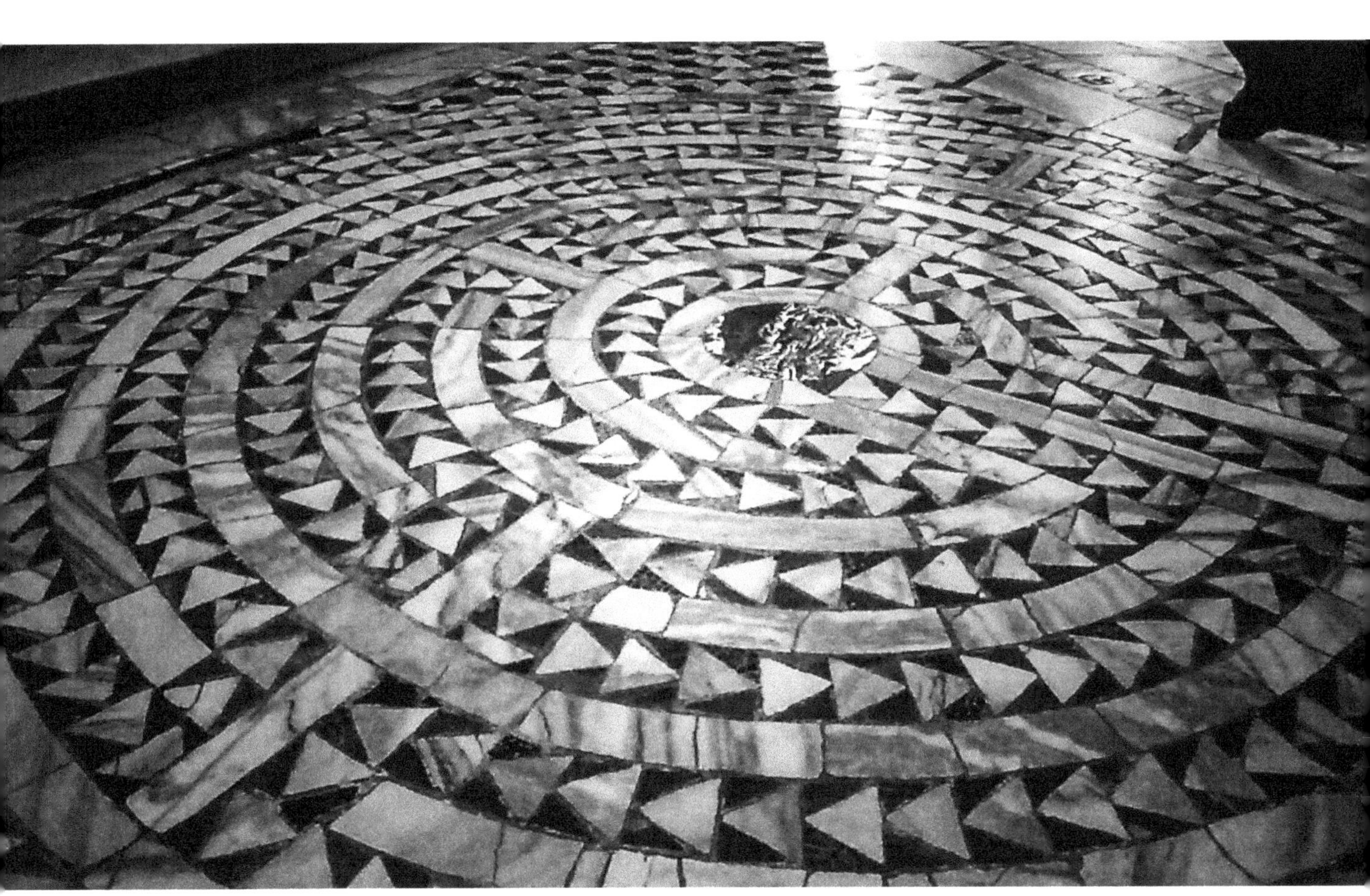

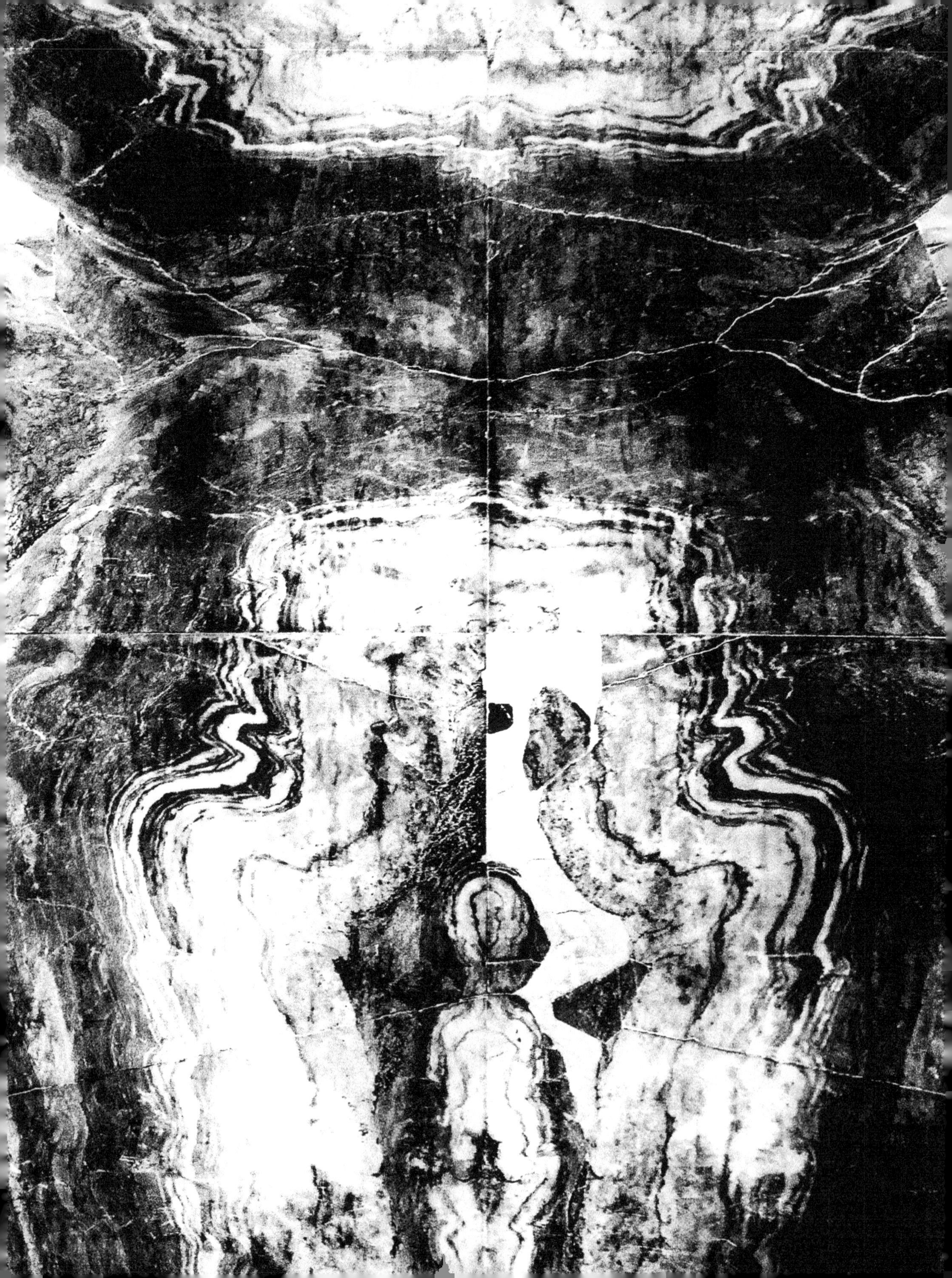

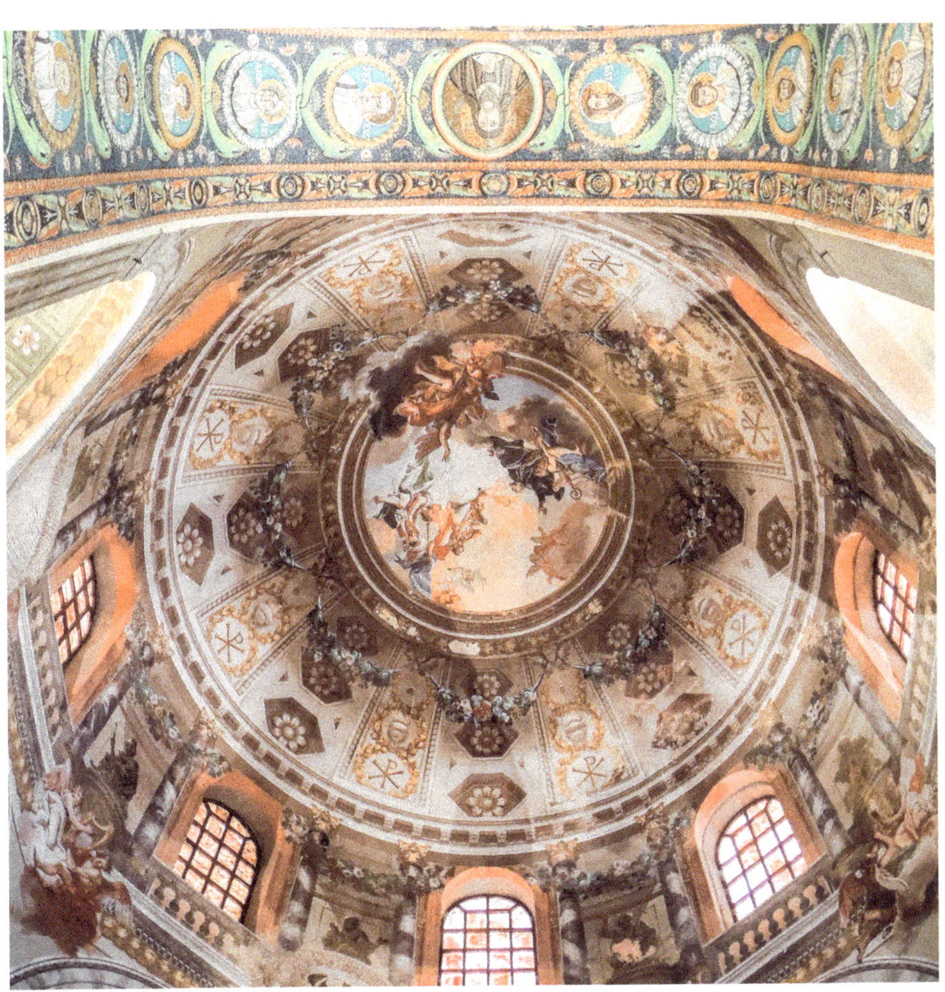

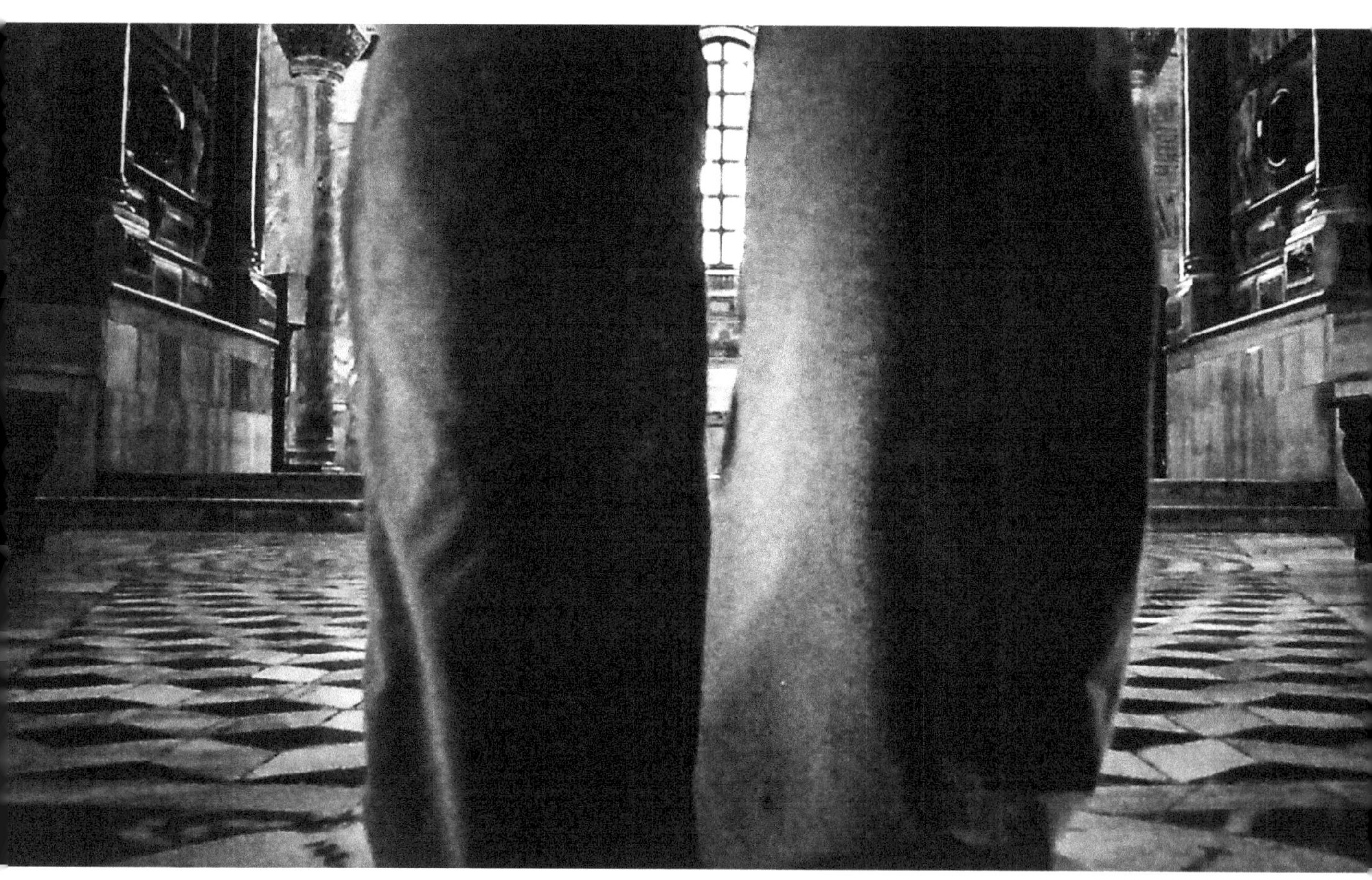

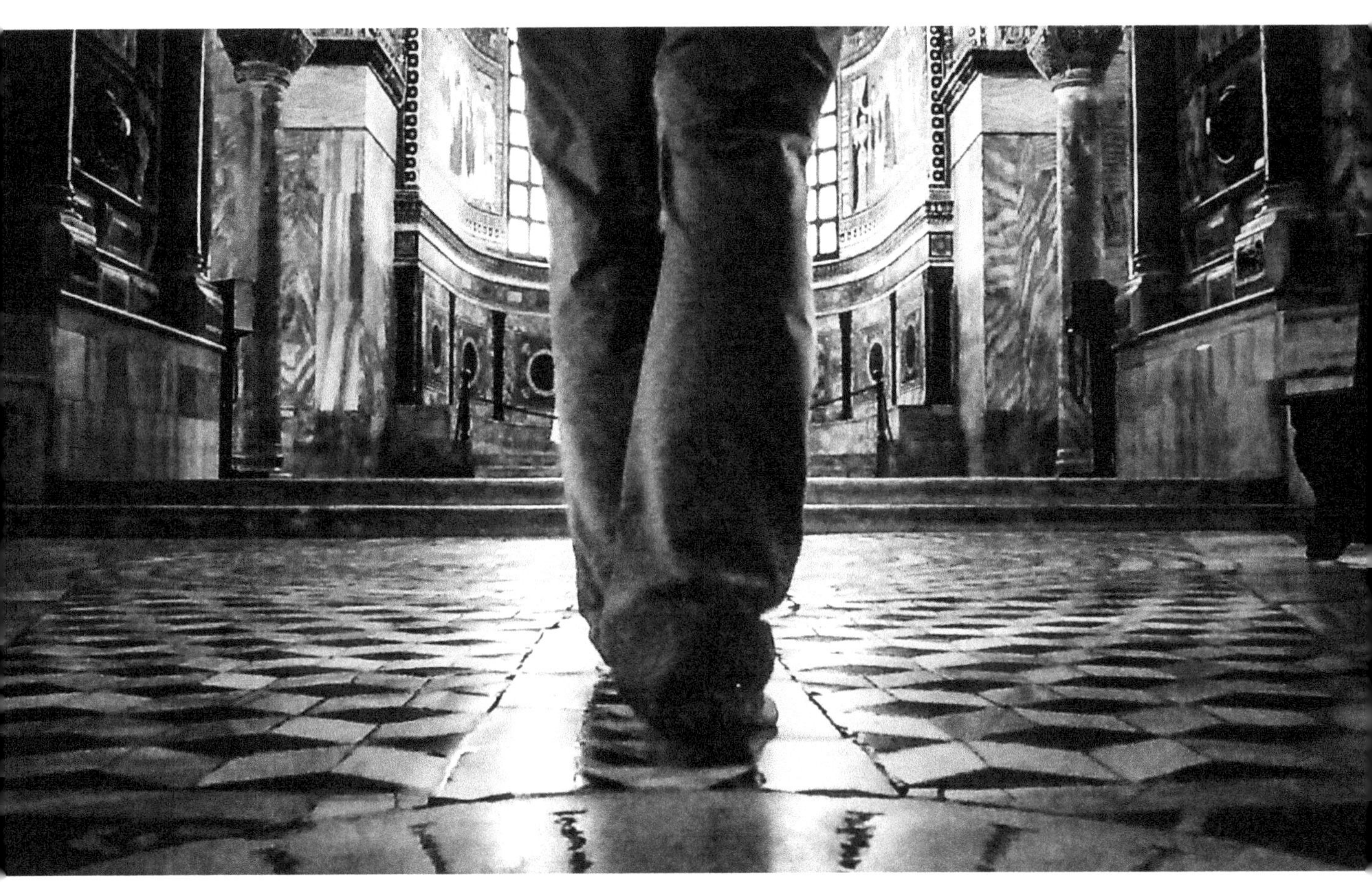

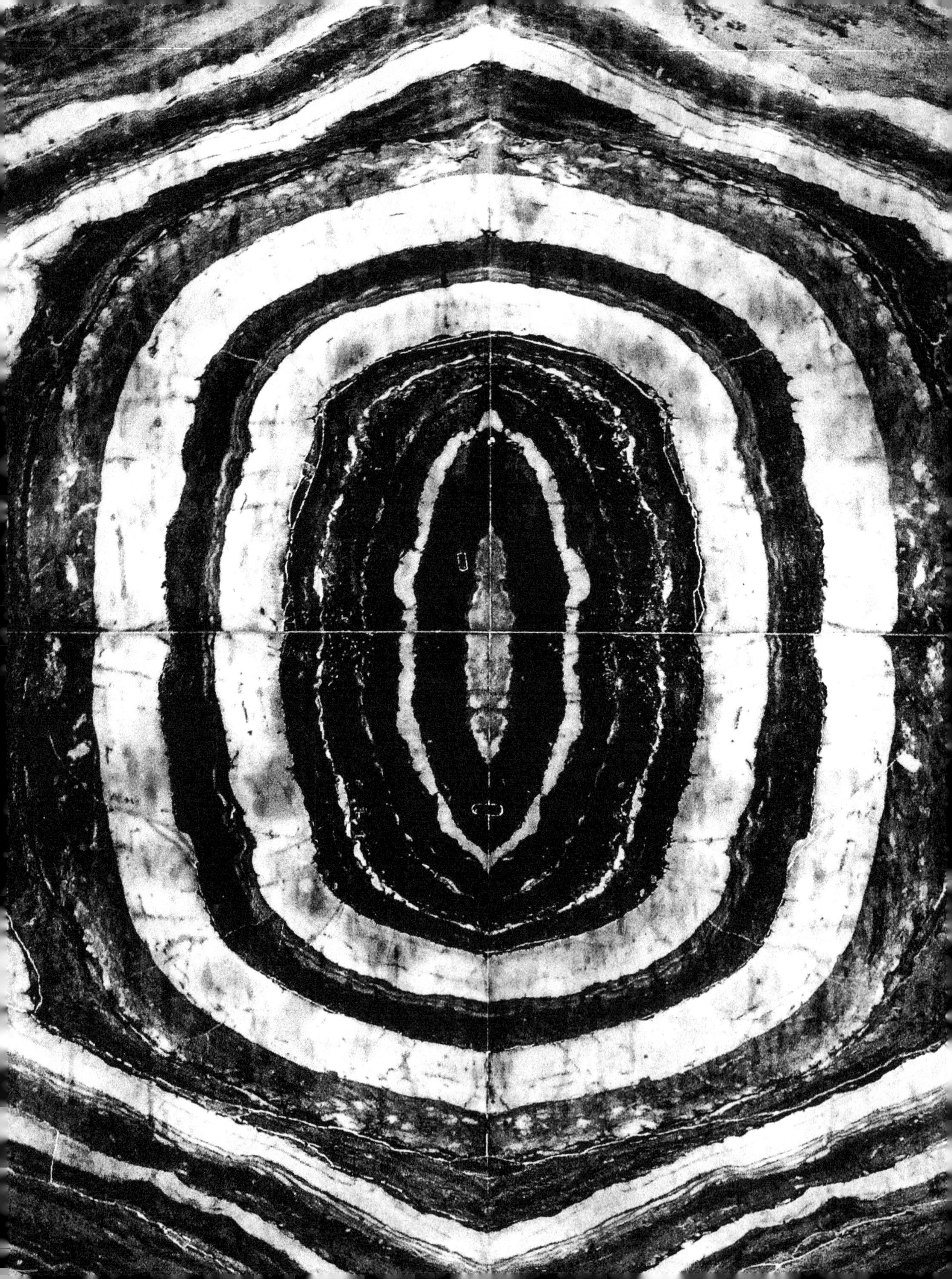

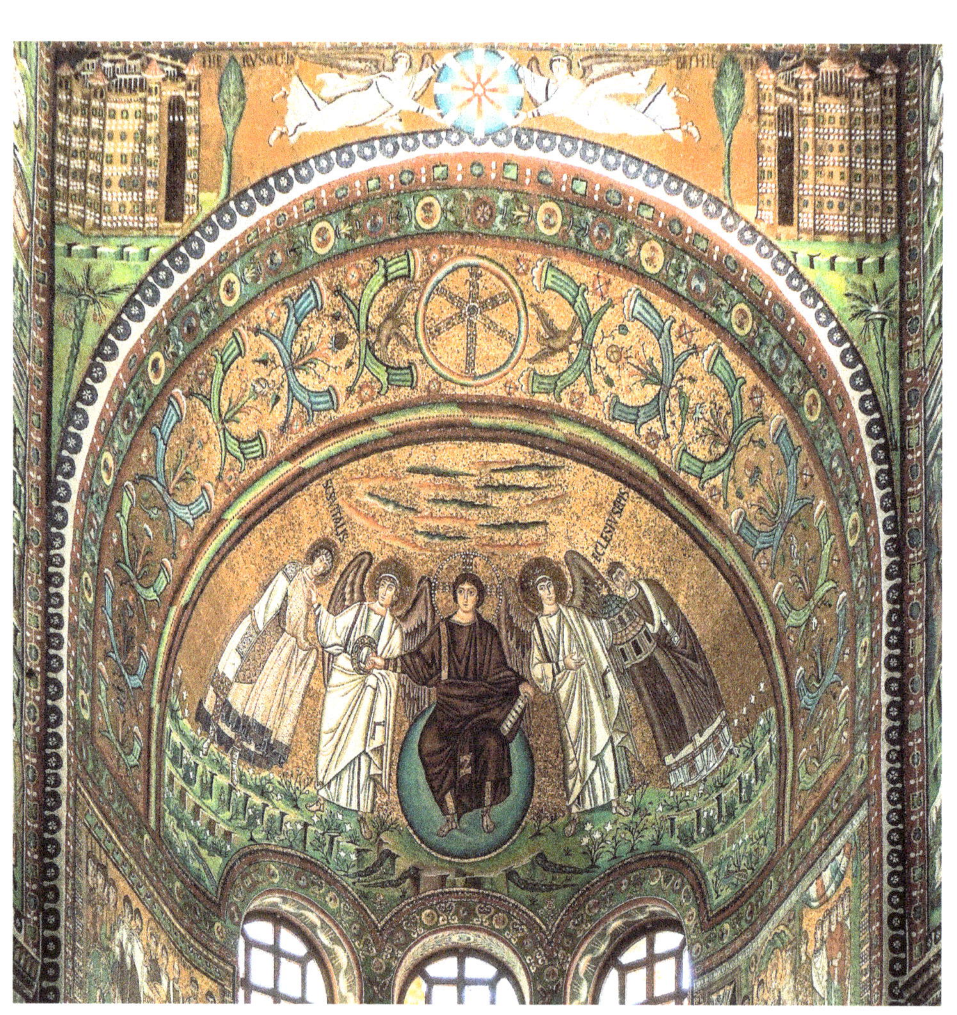

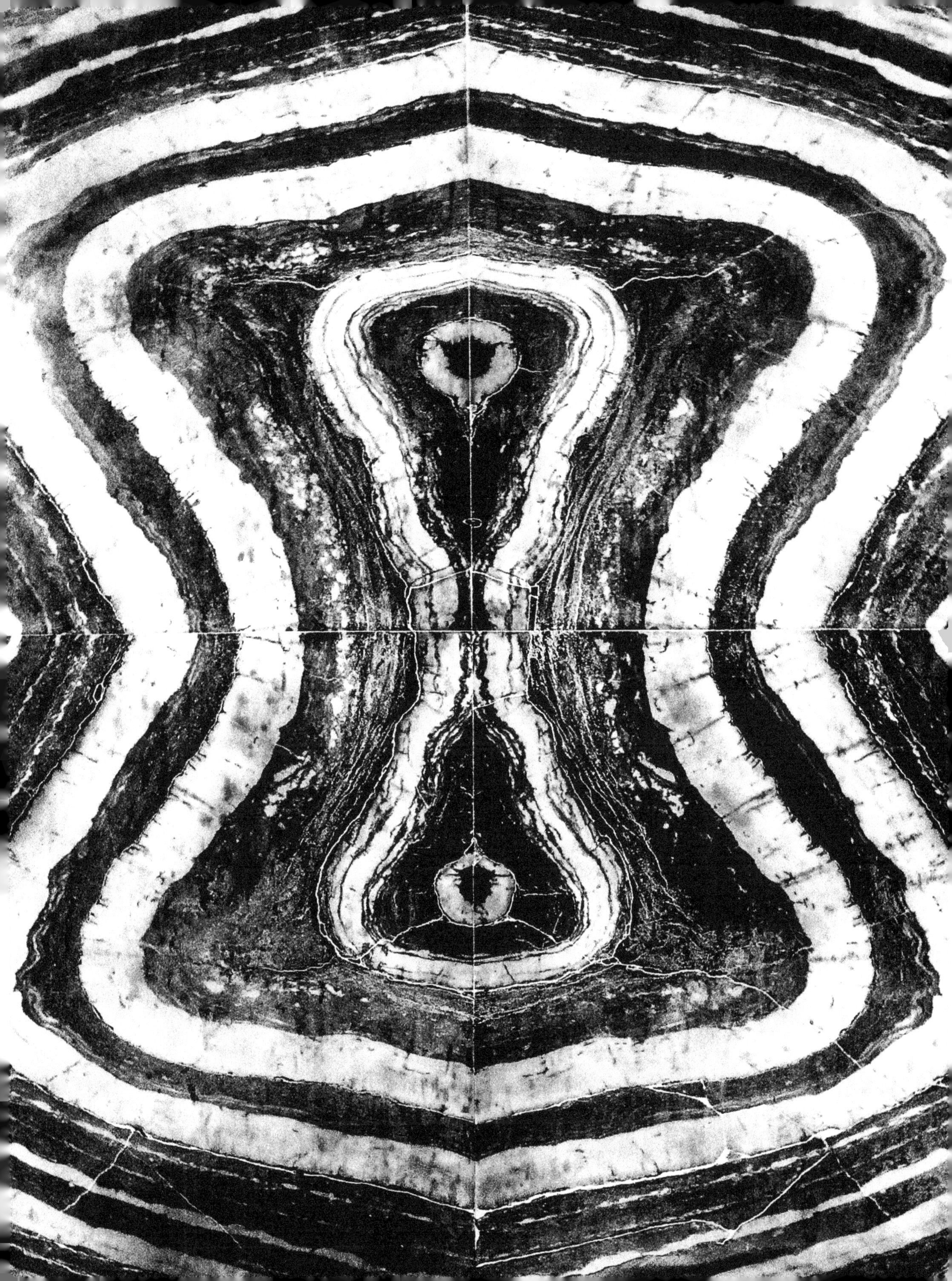

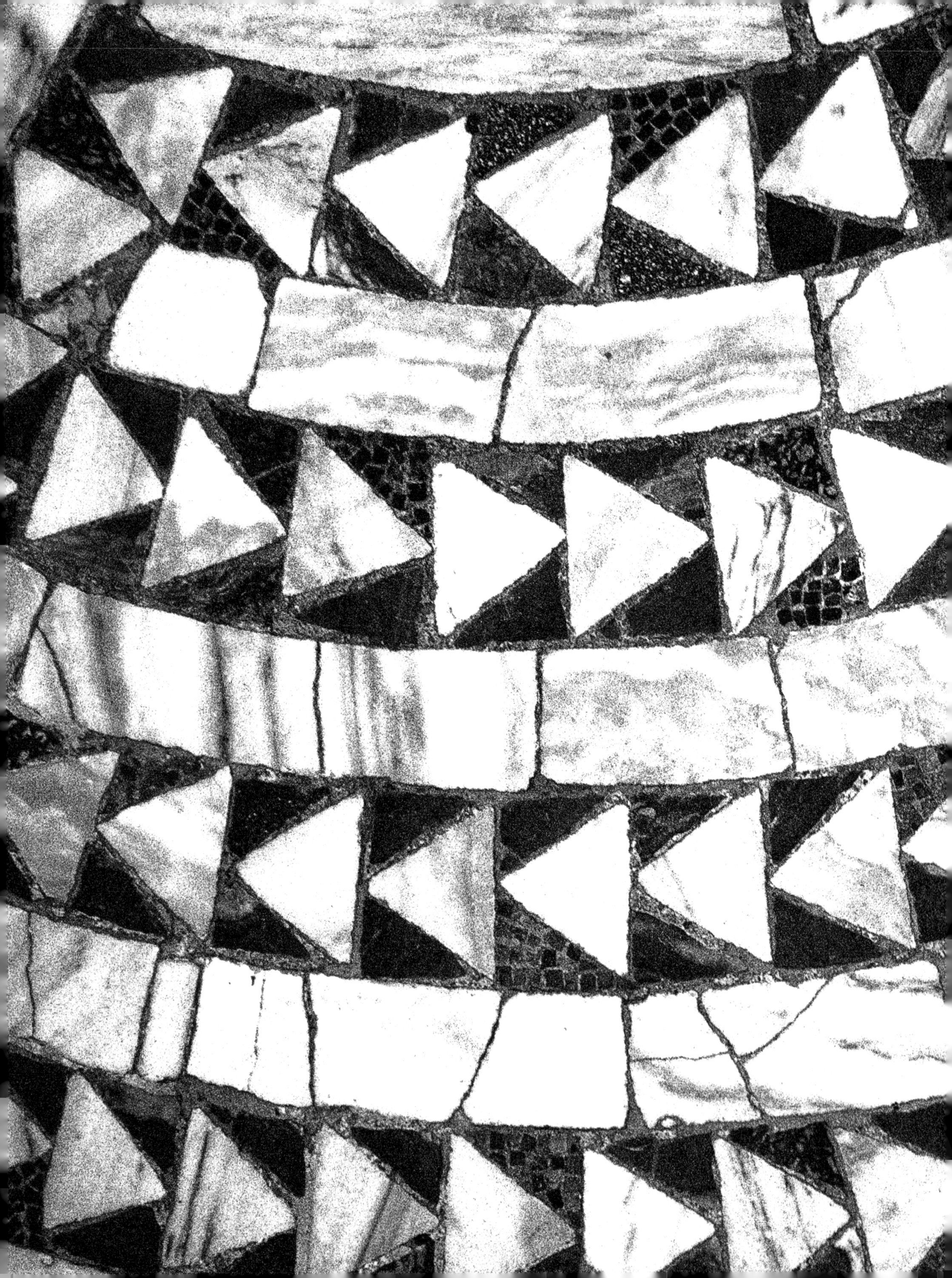

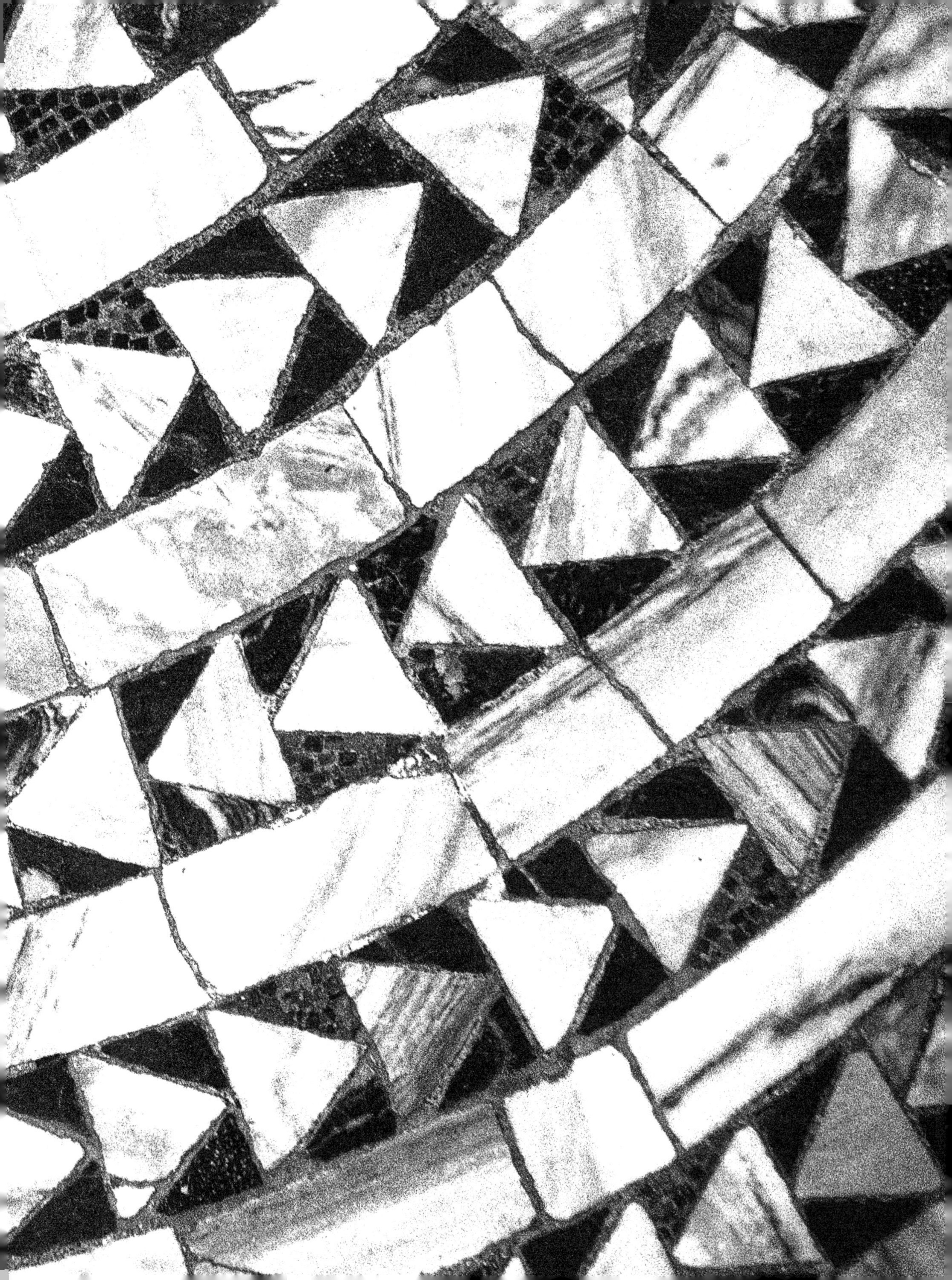

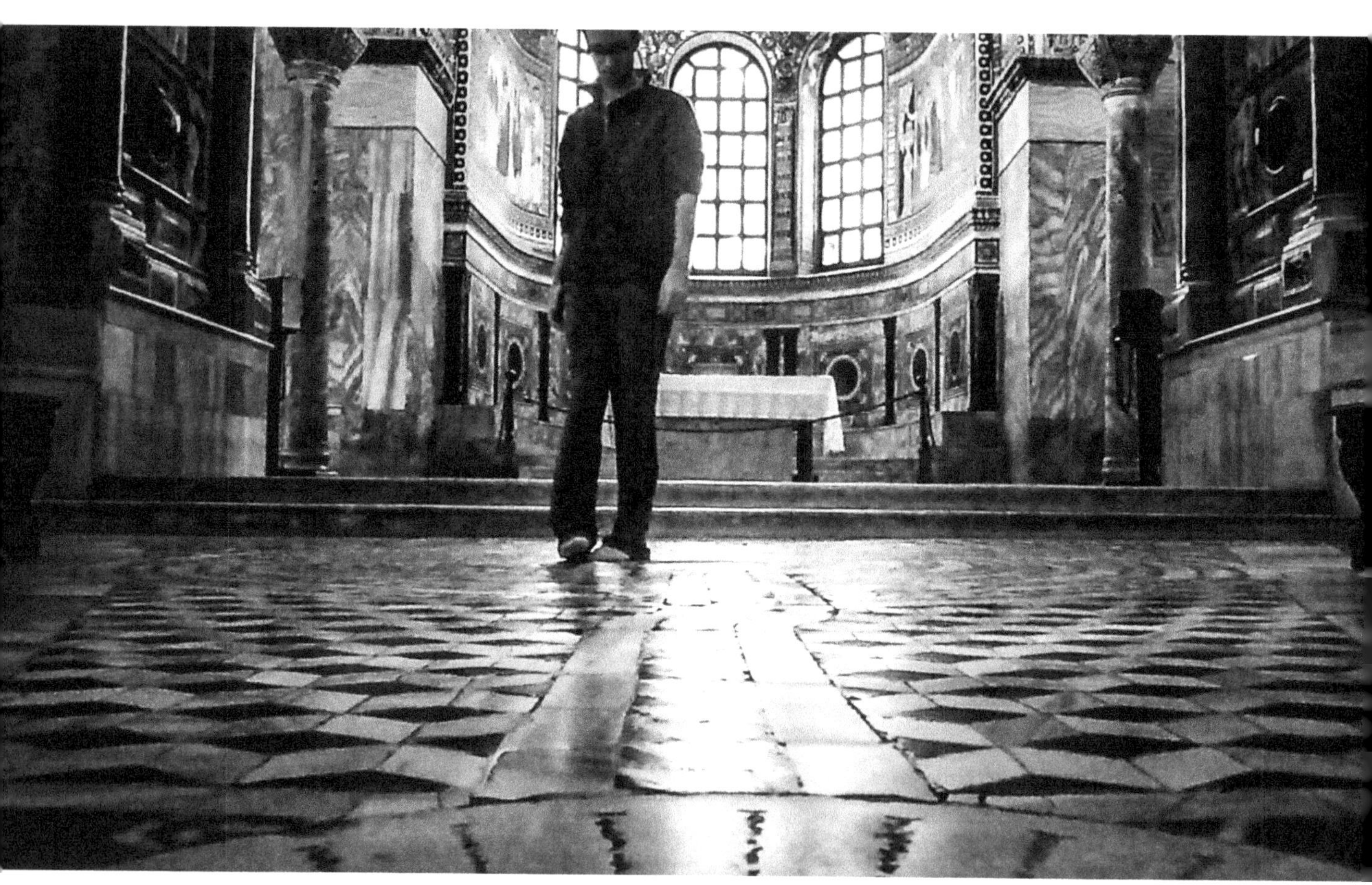

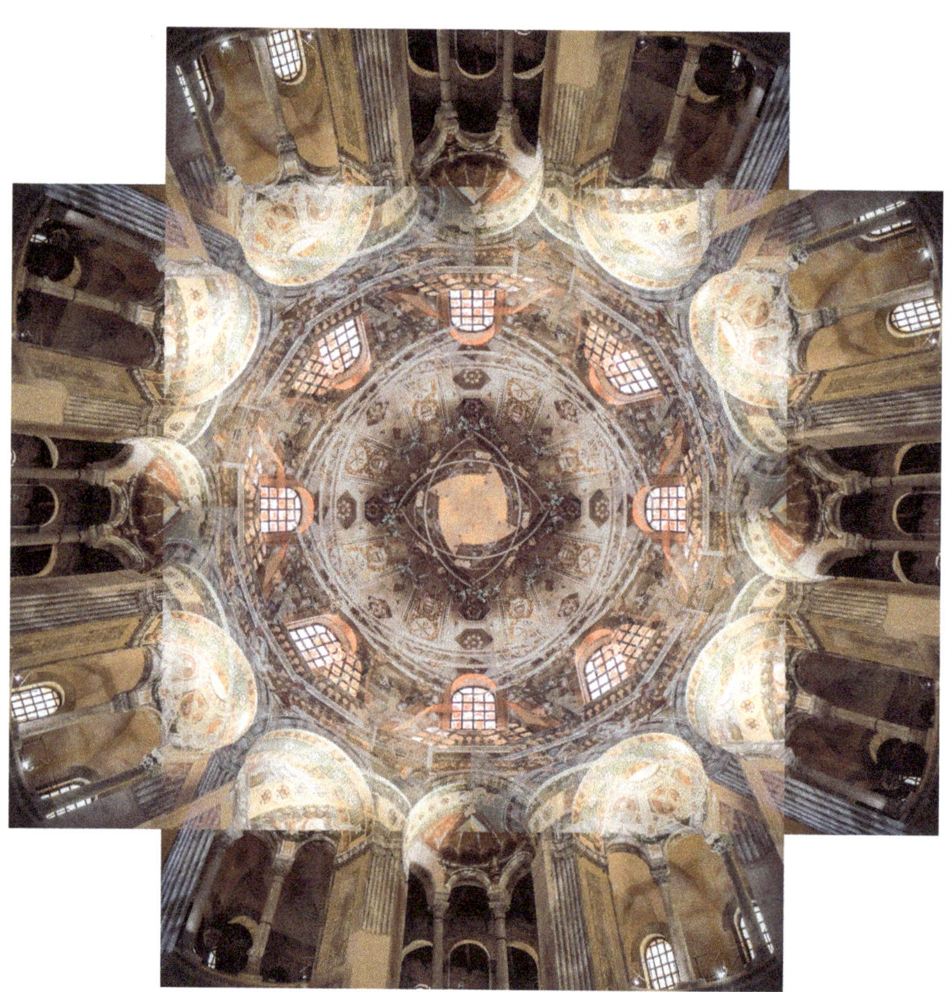

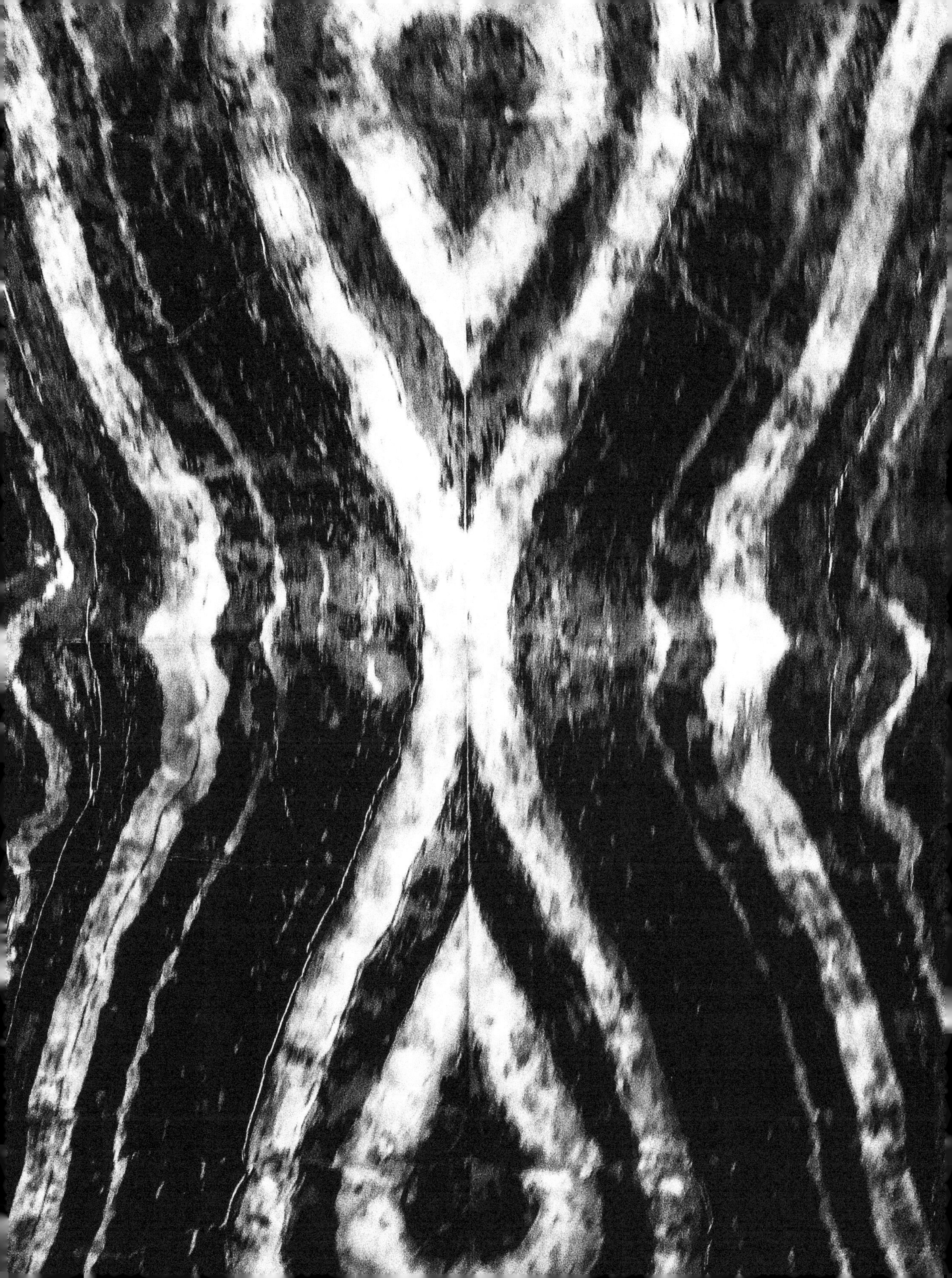

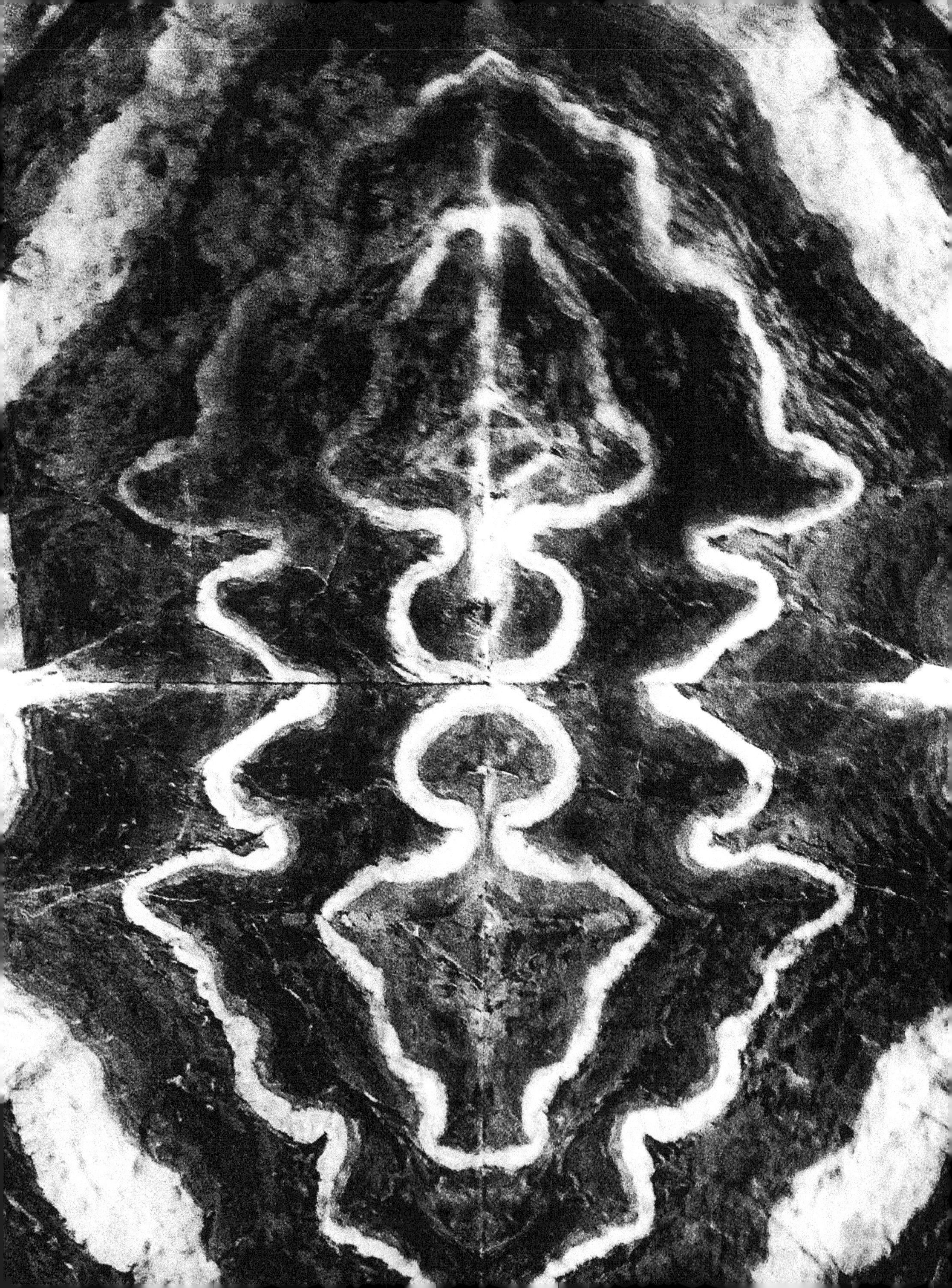

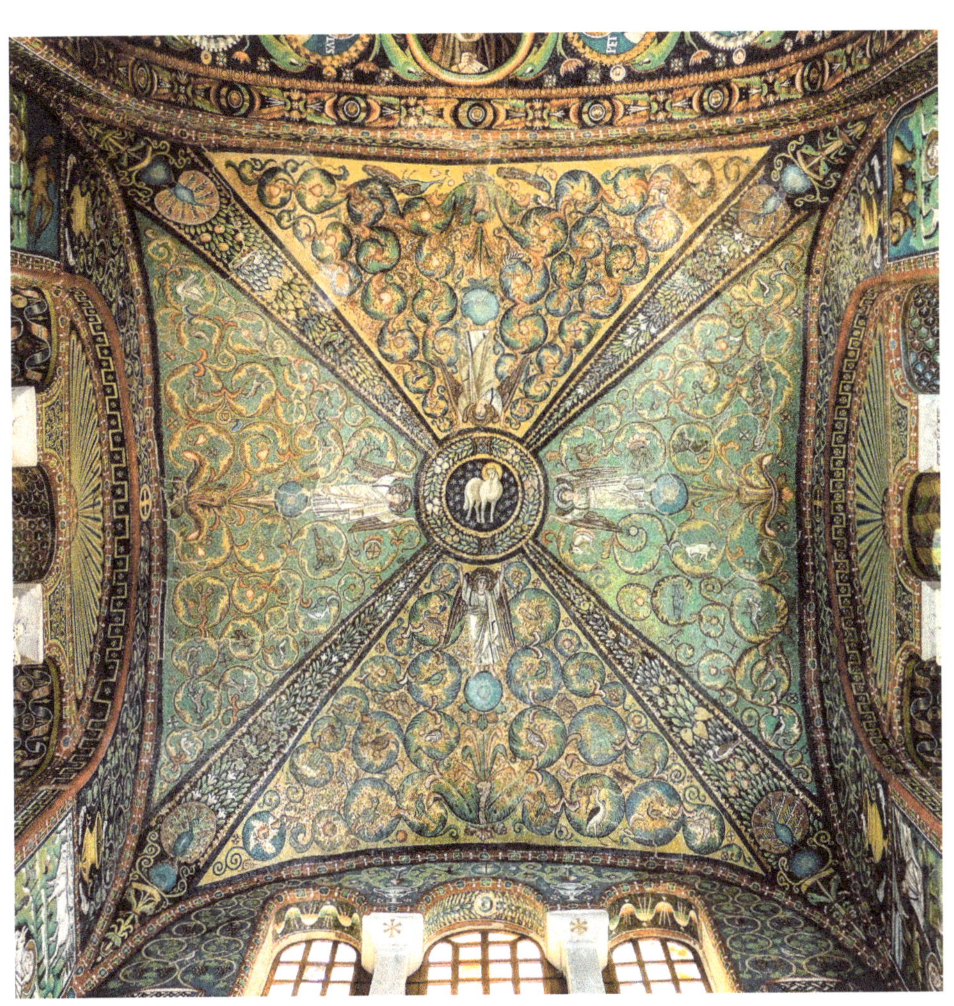

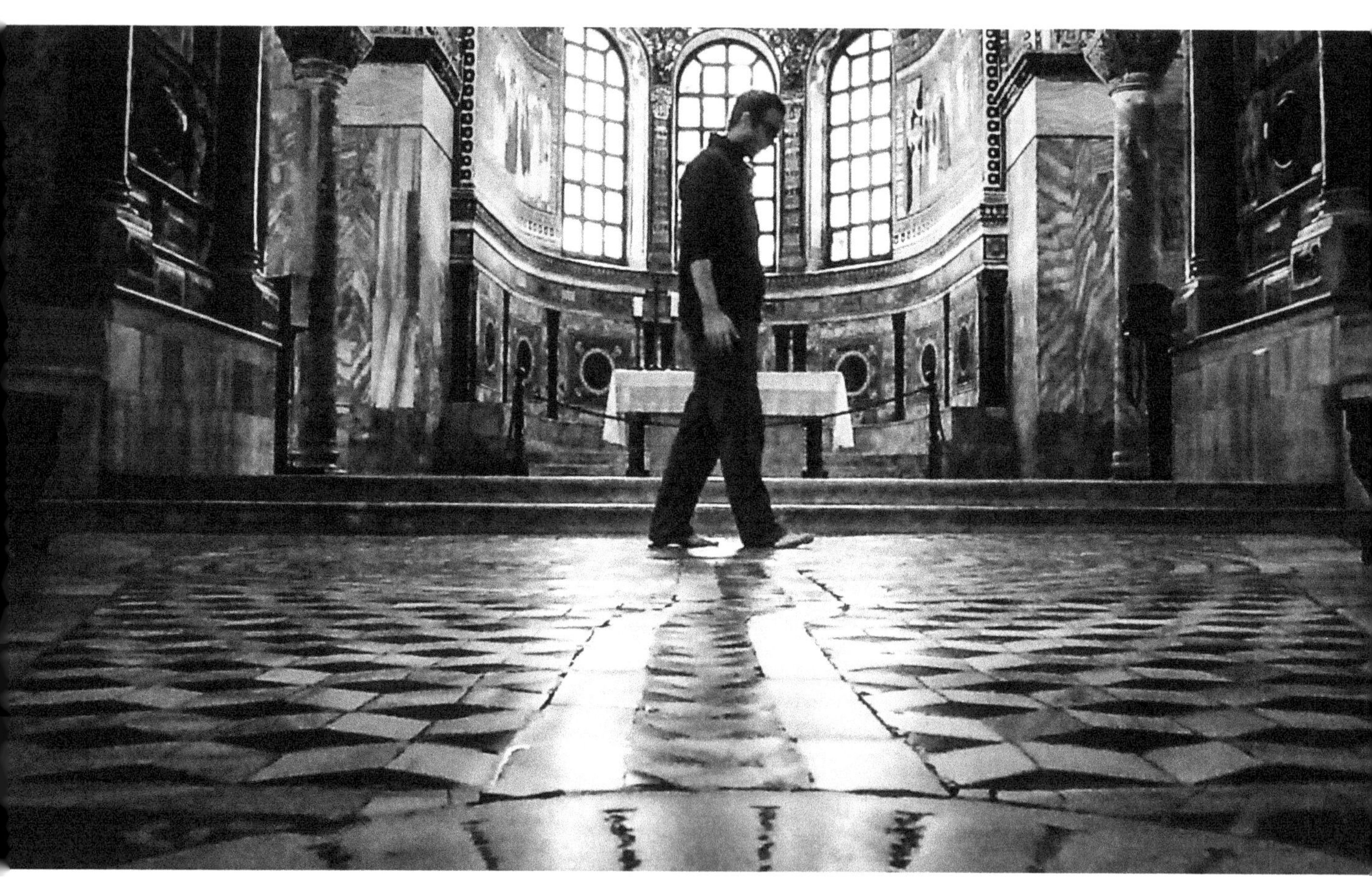

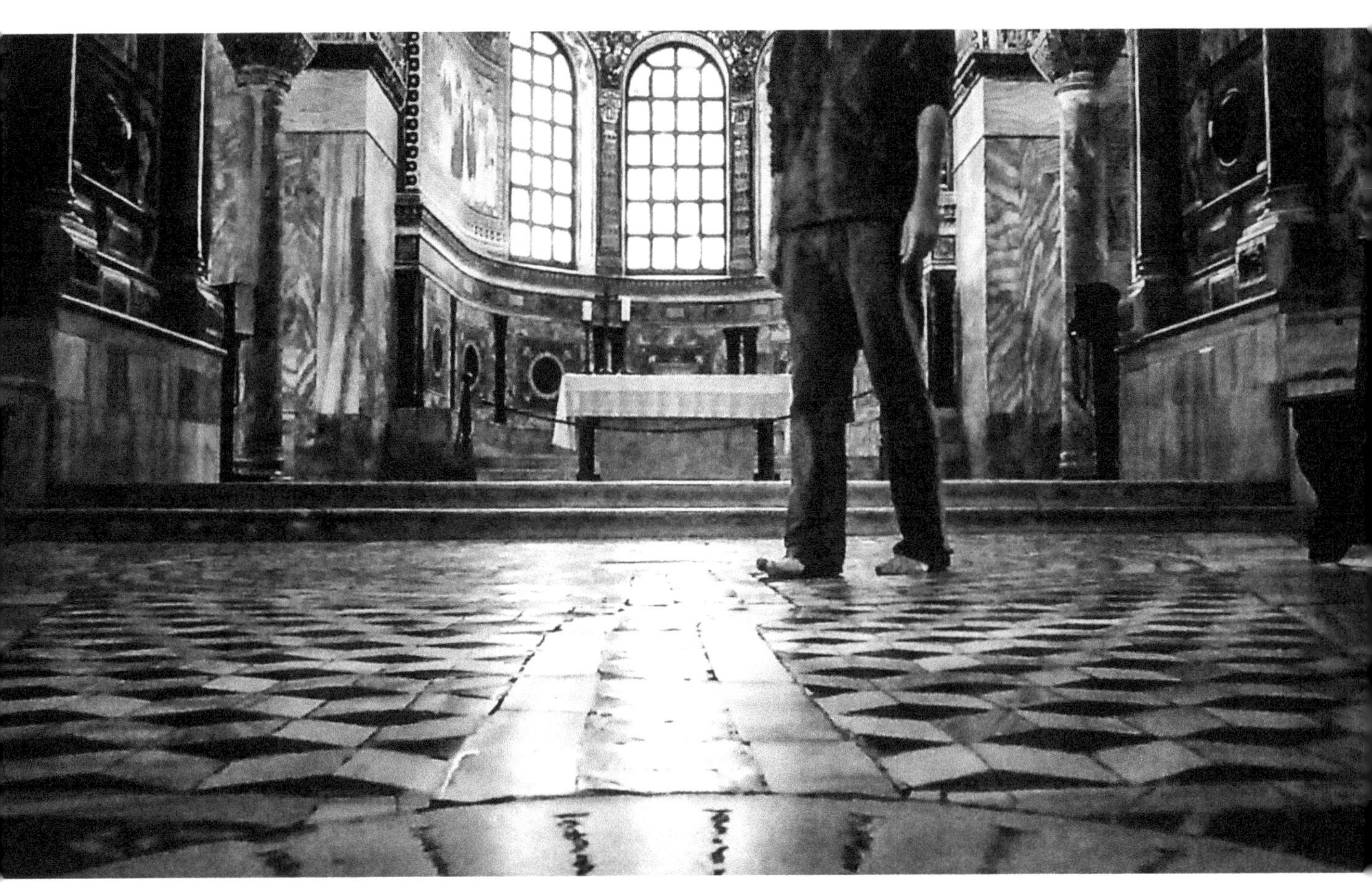

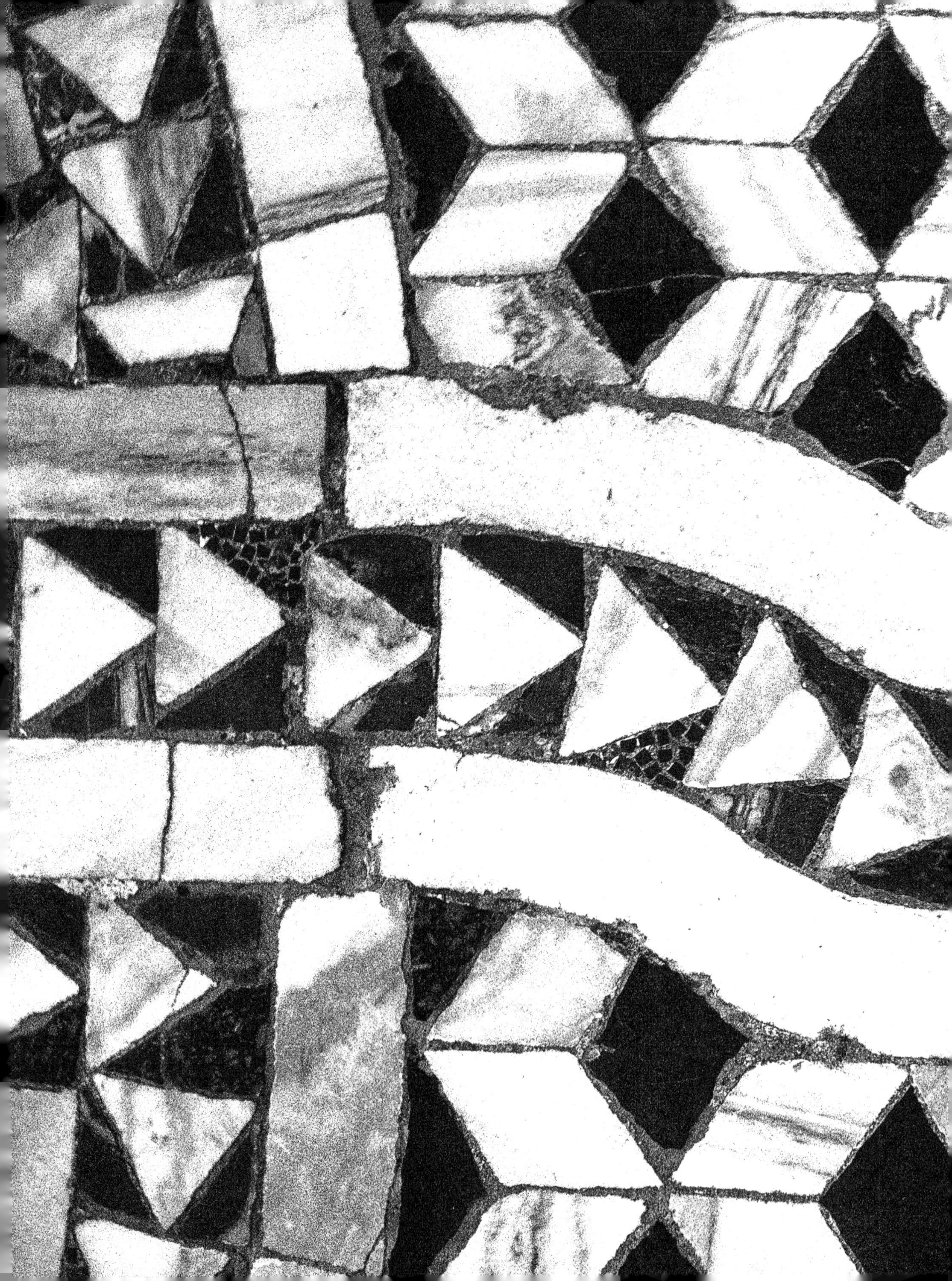

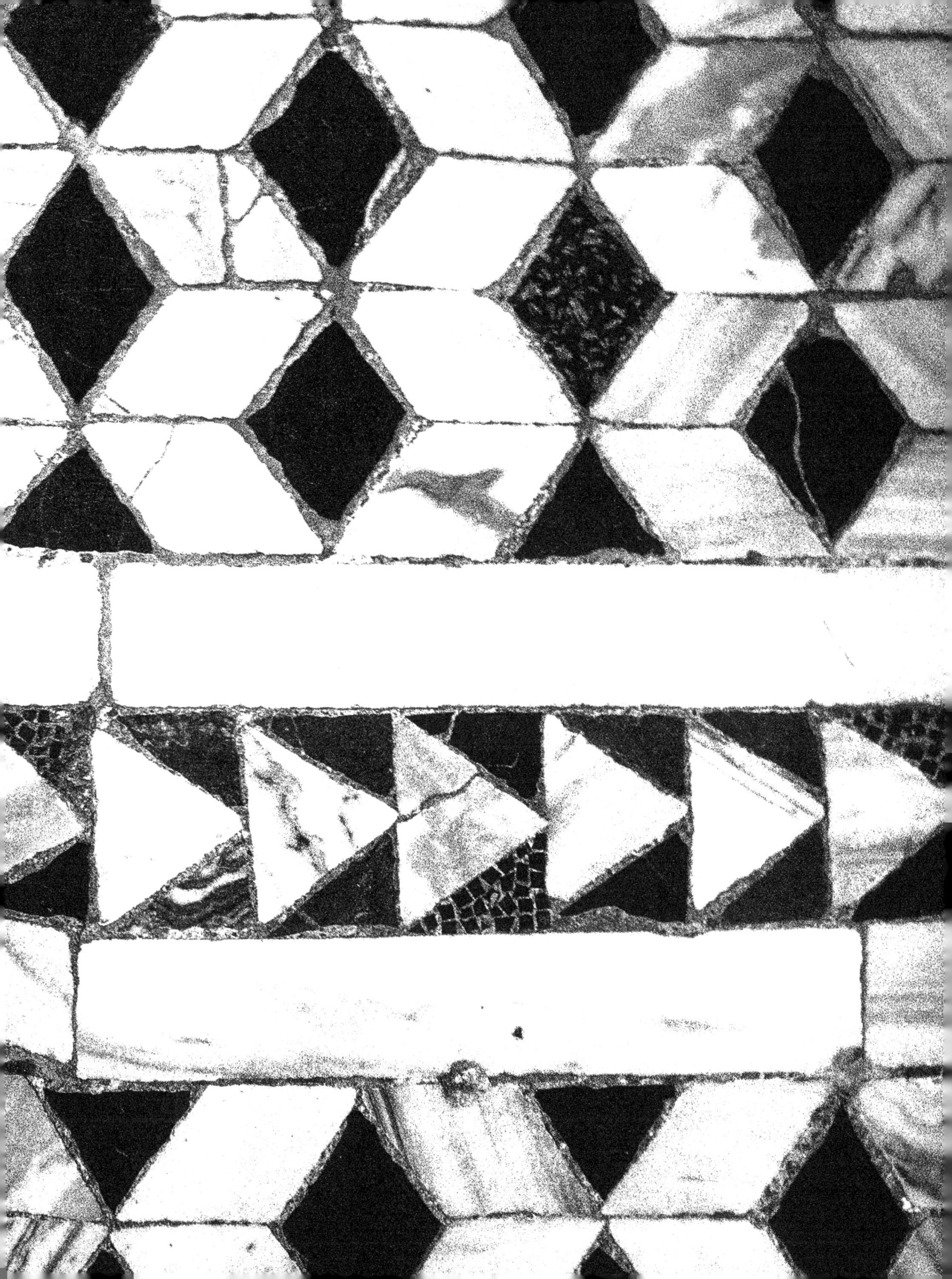

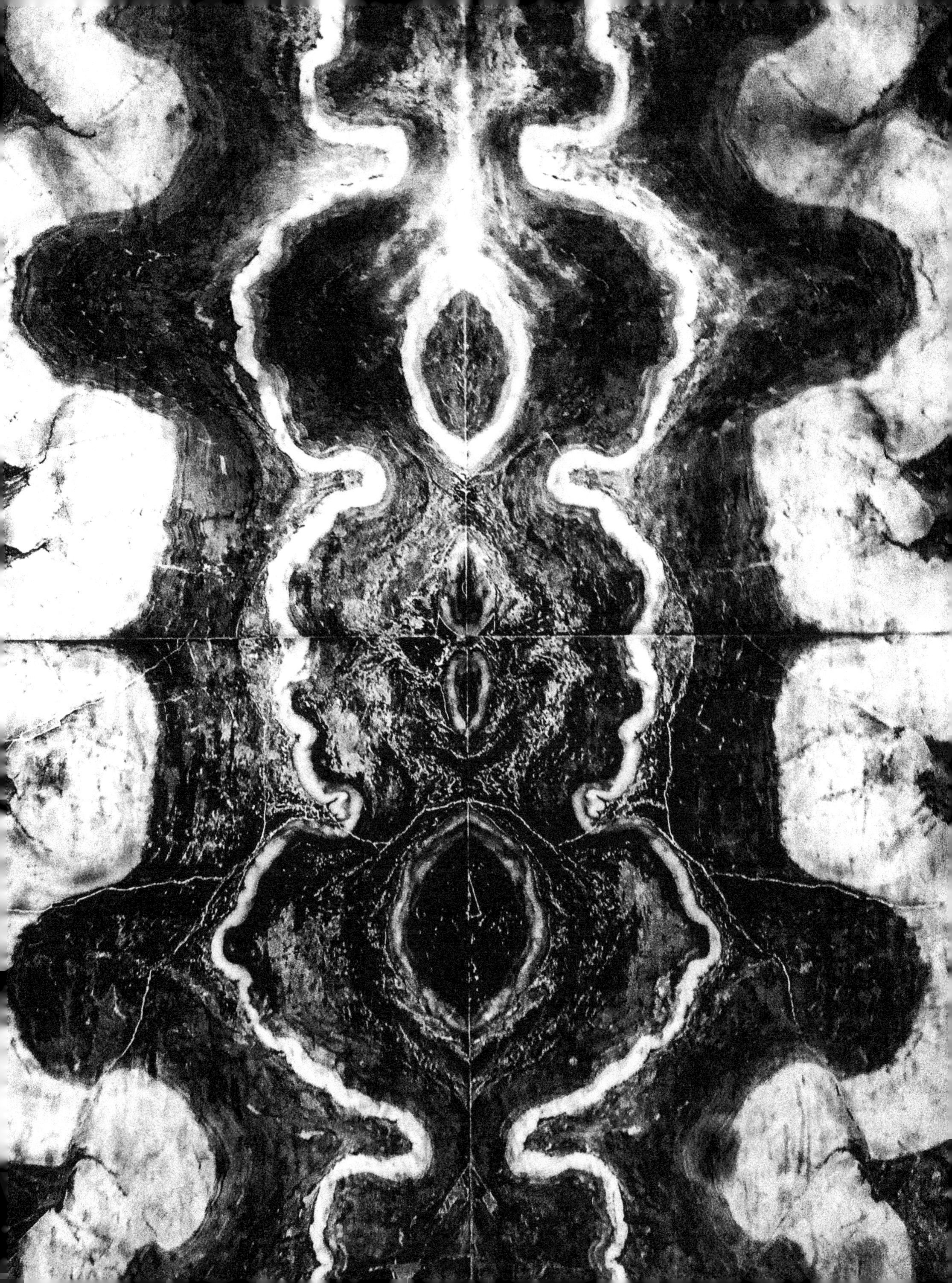

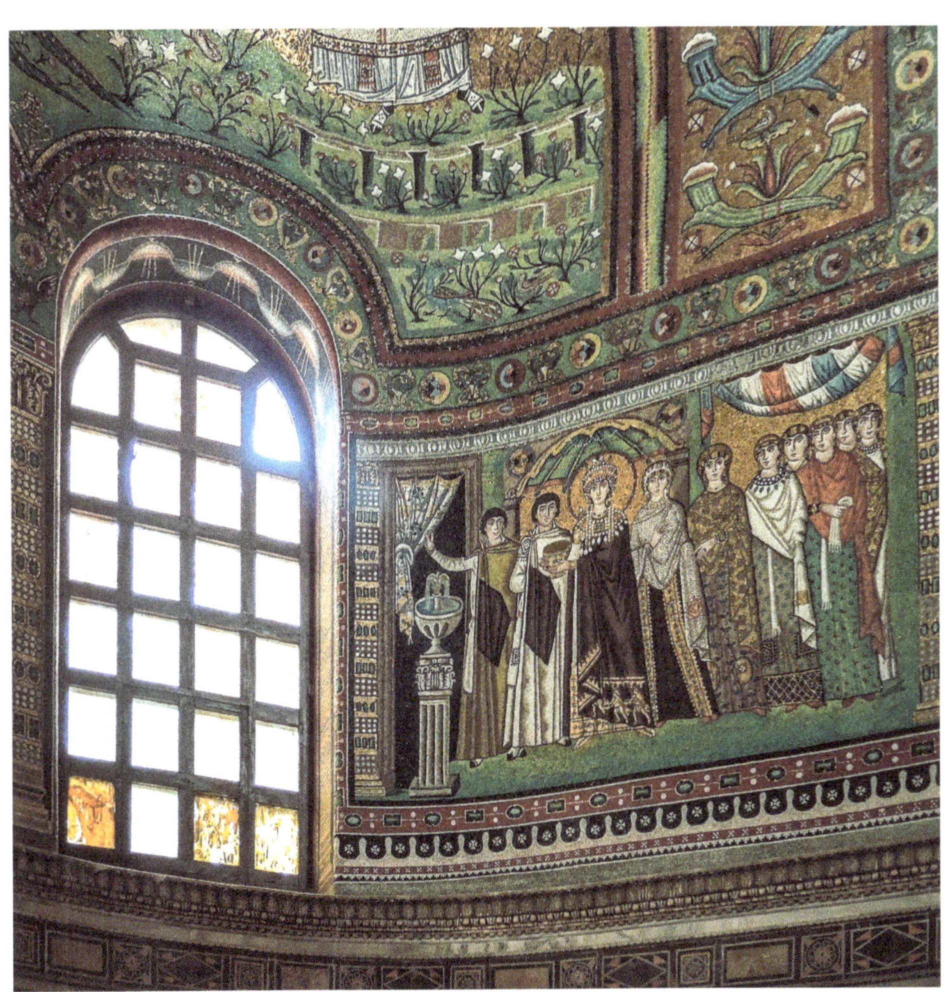

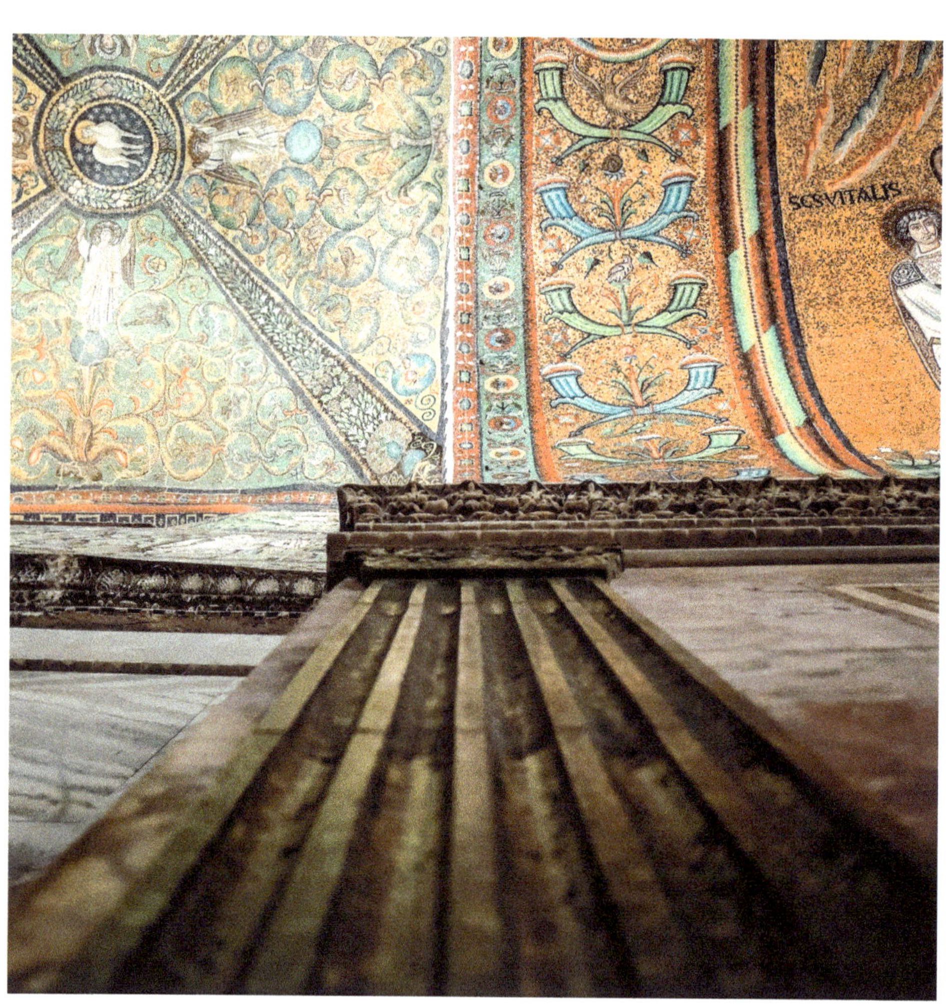
SCS VITALIS

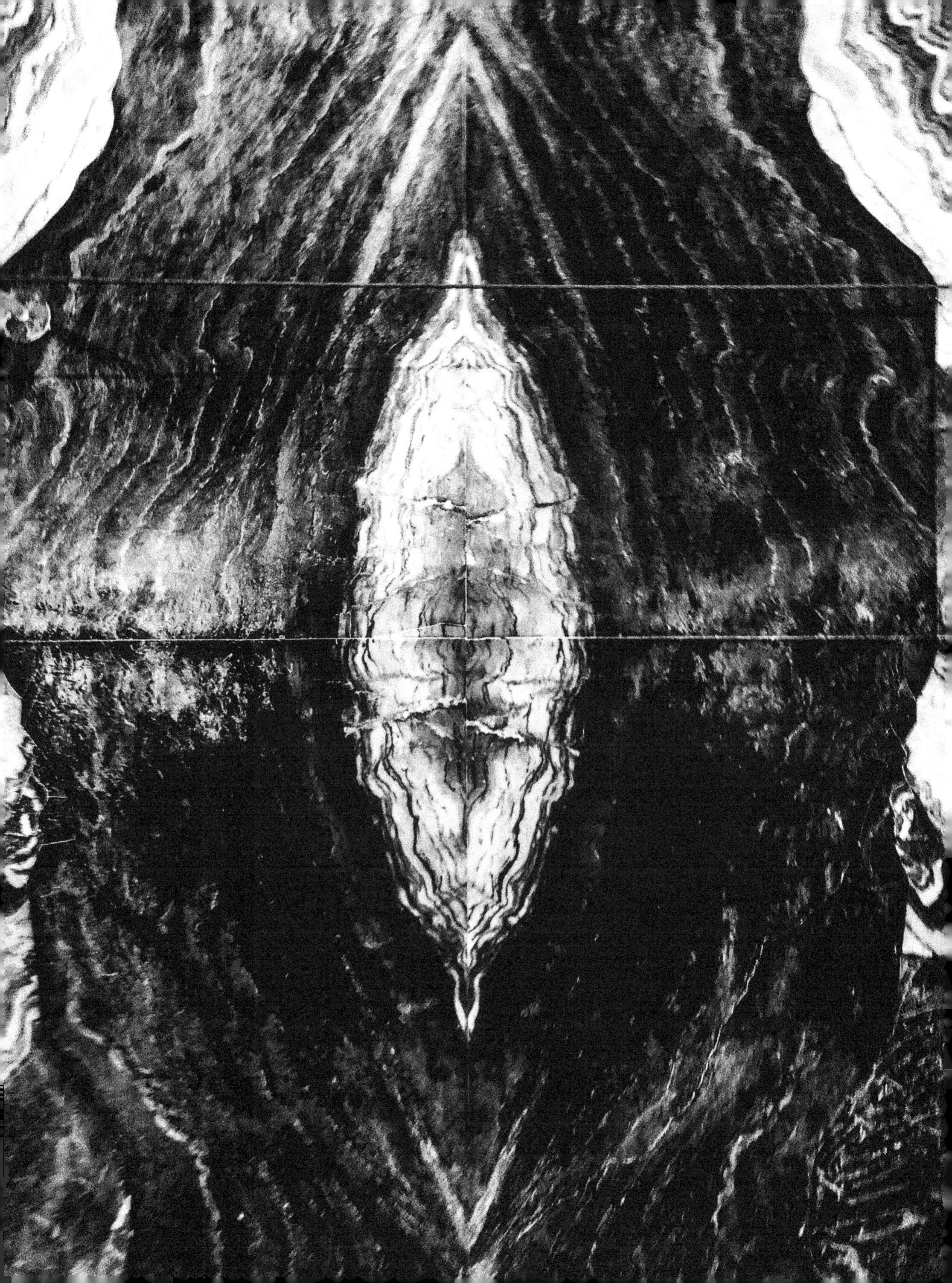

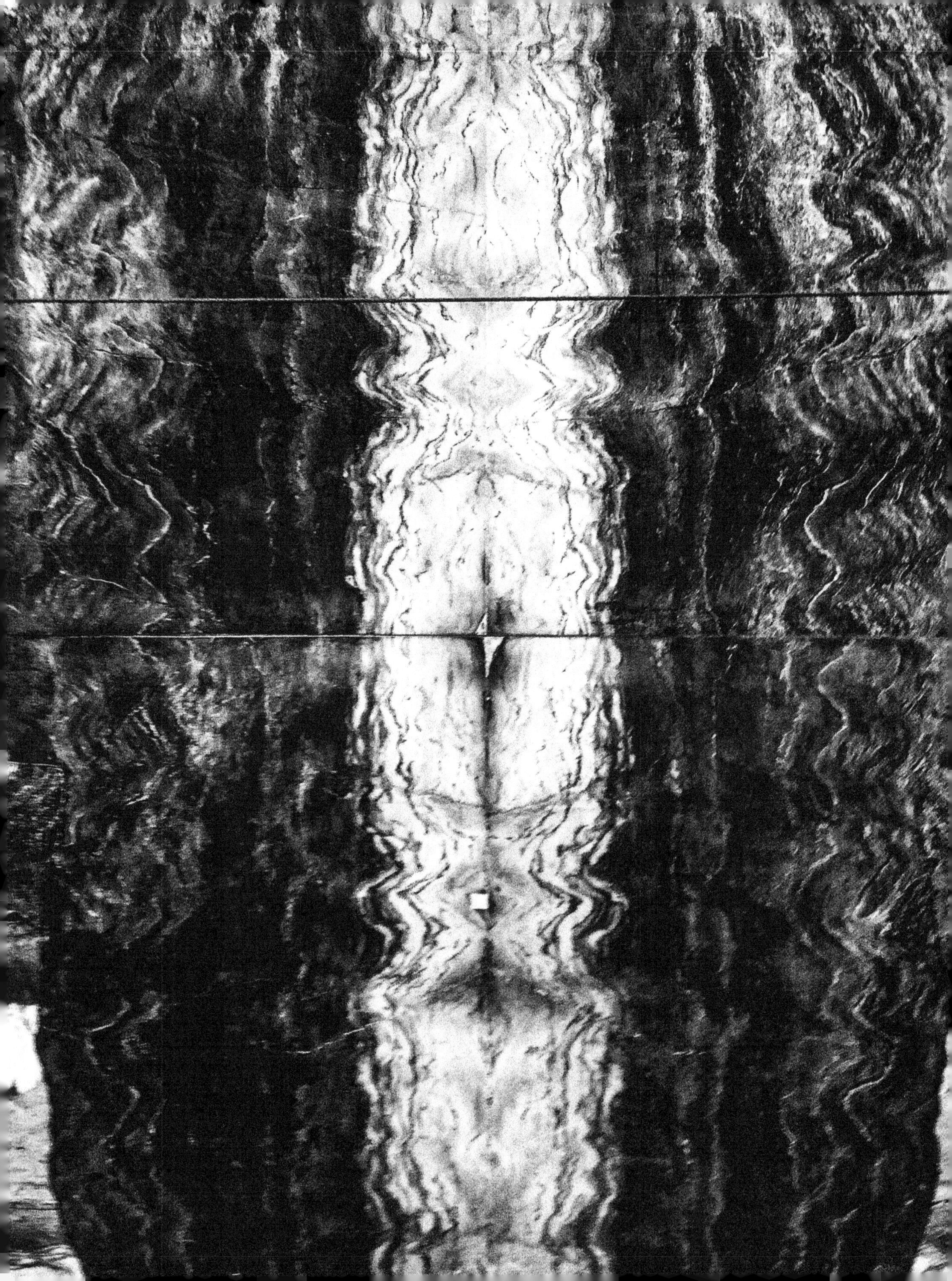

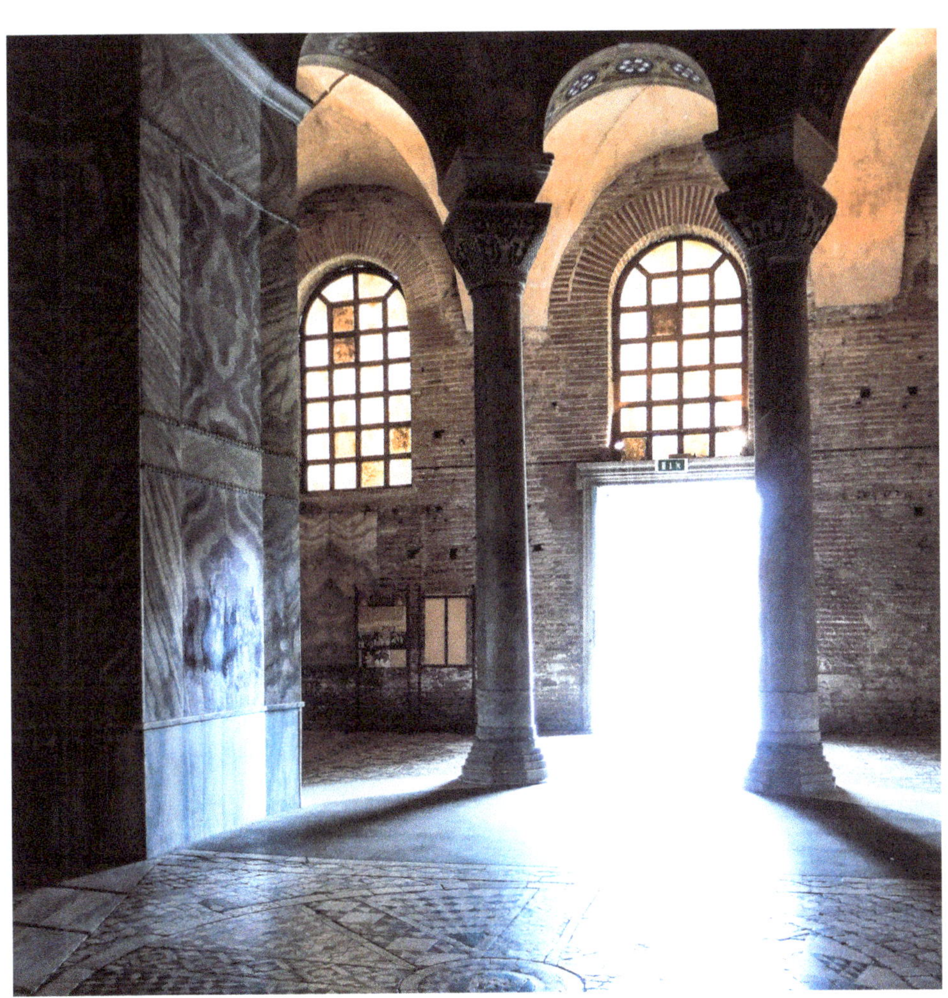

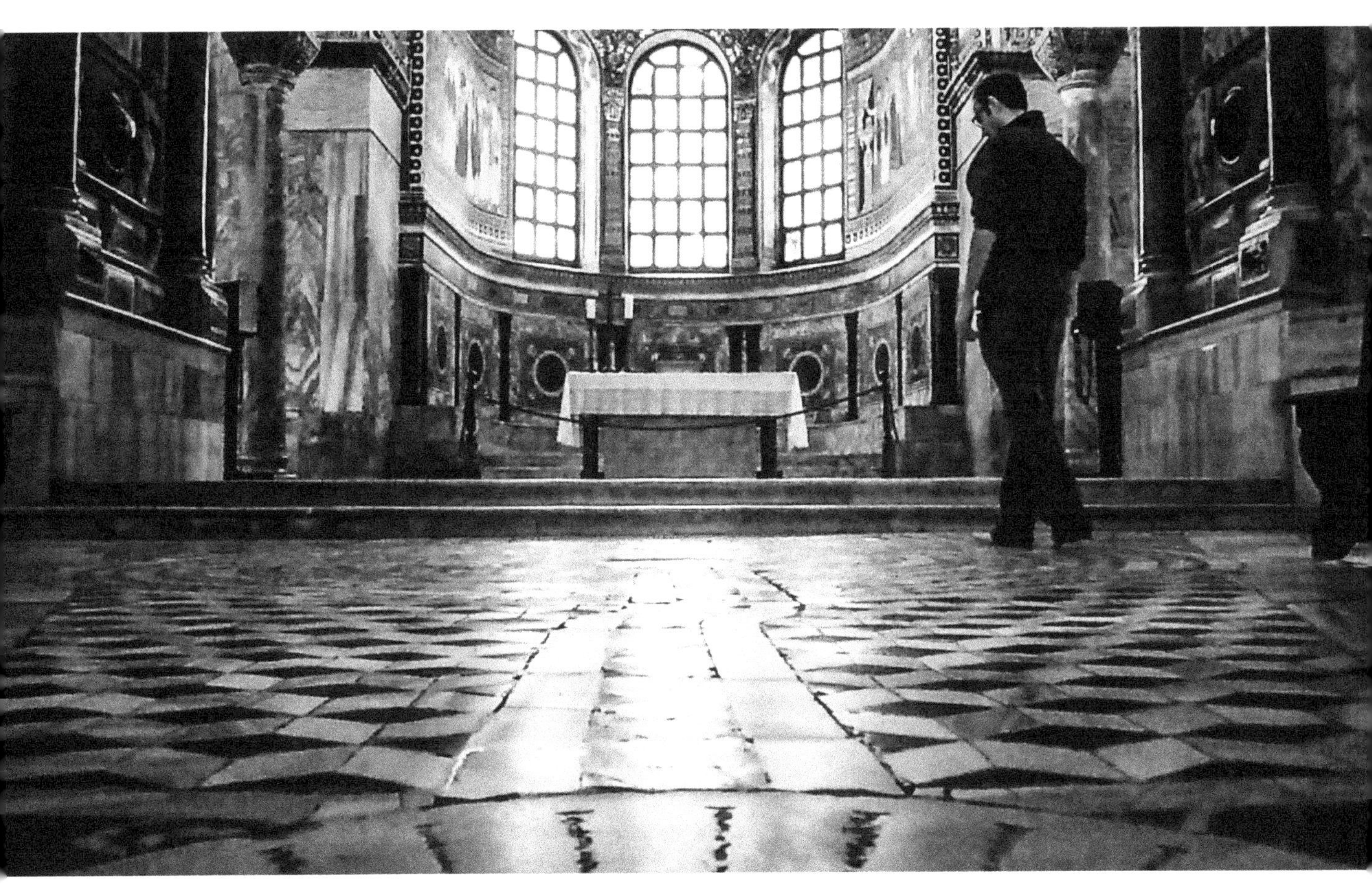

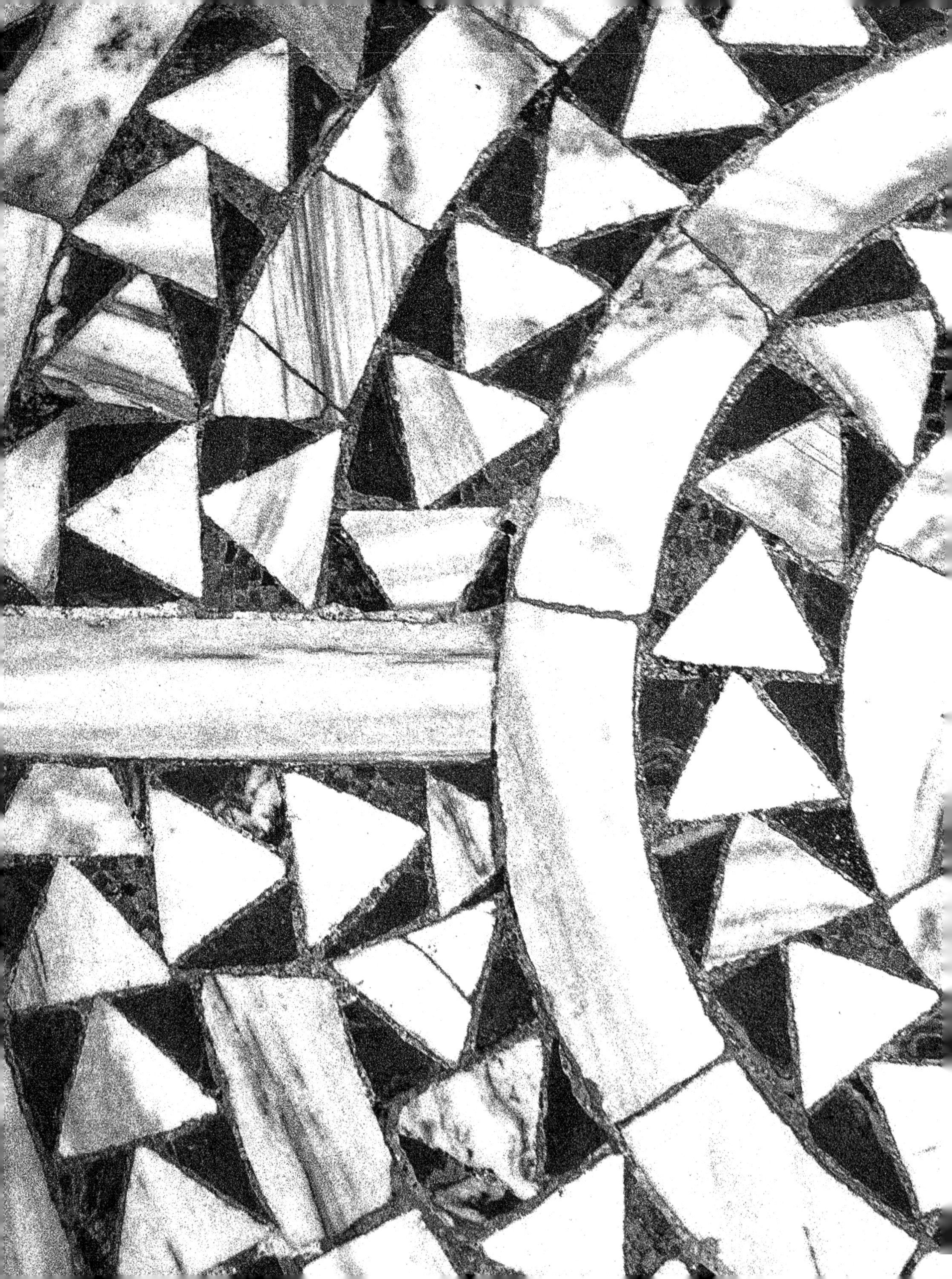

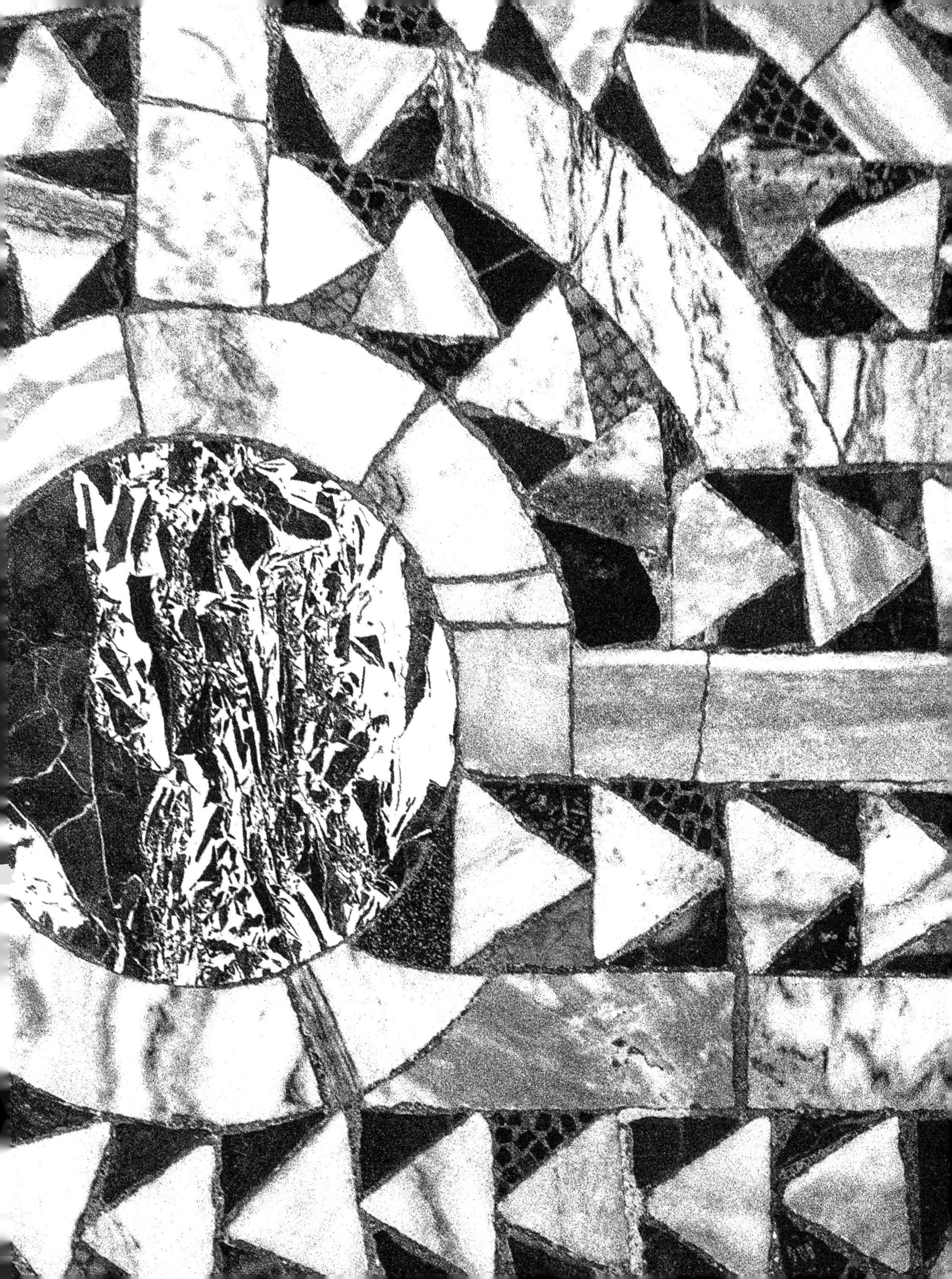

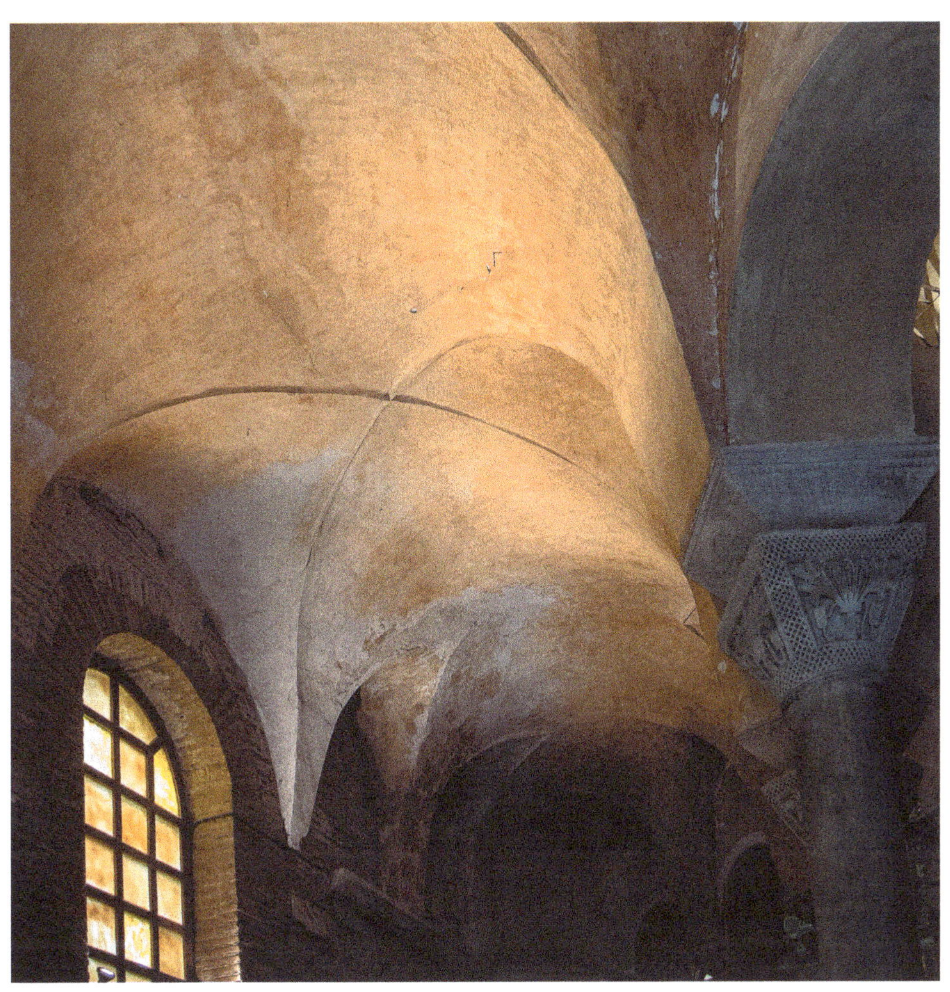

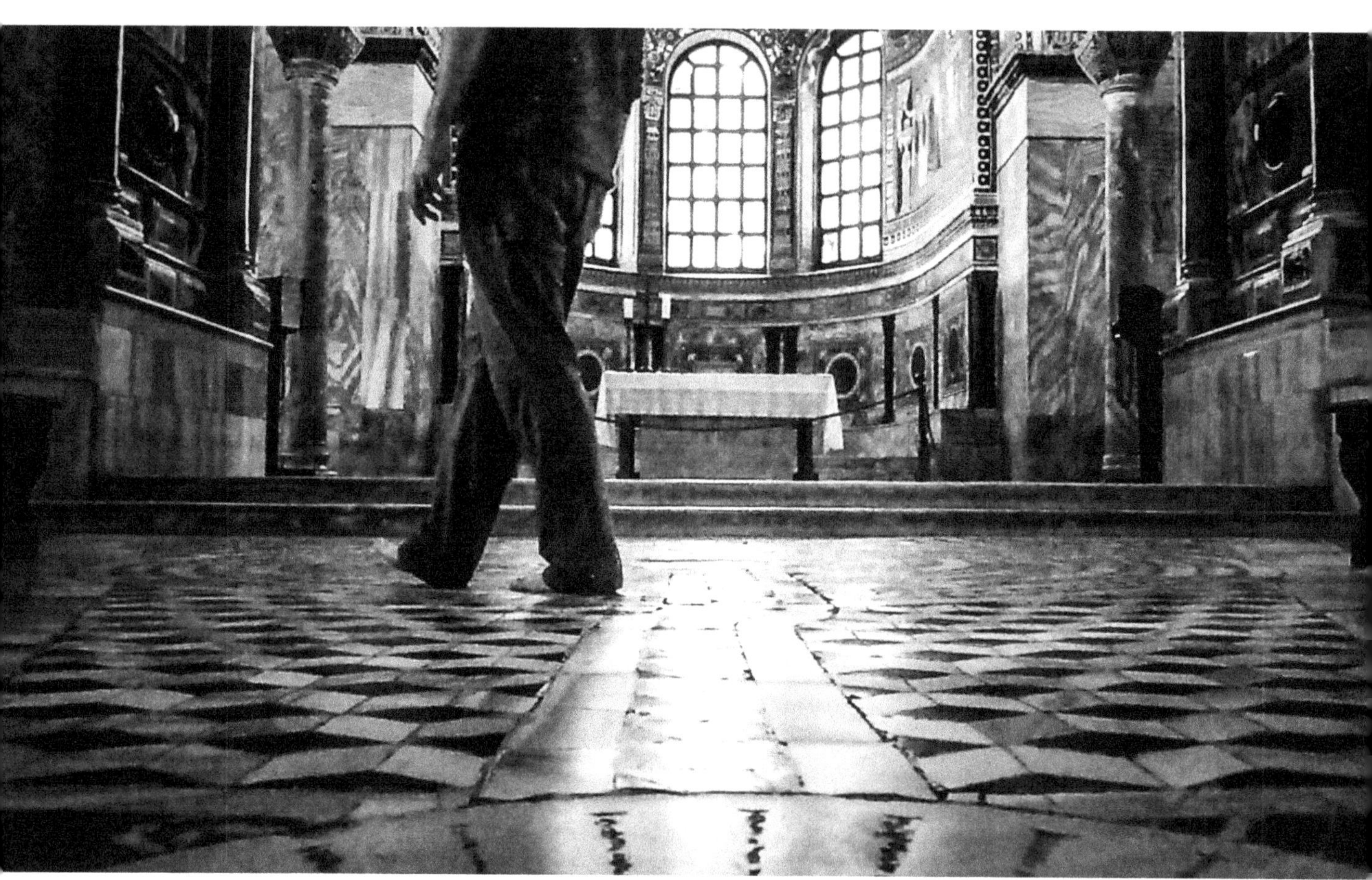

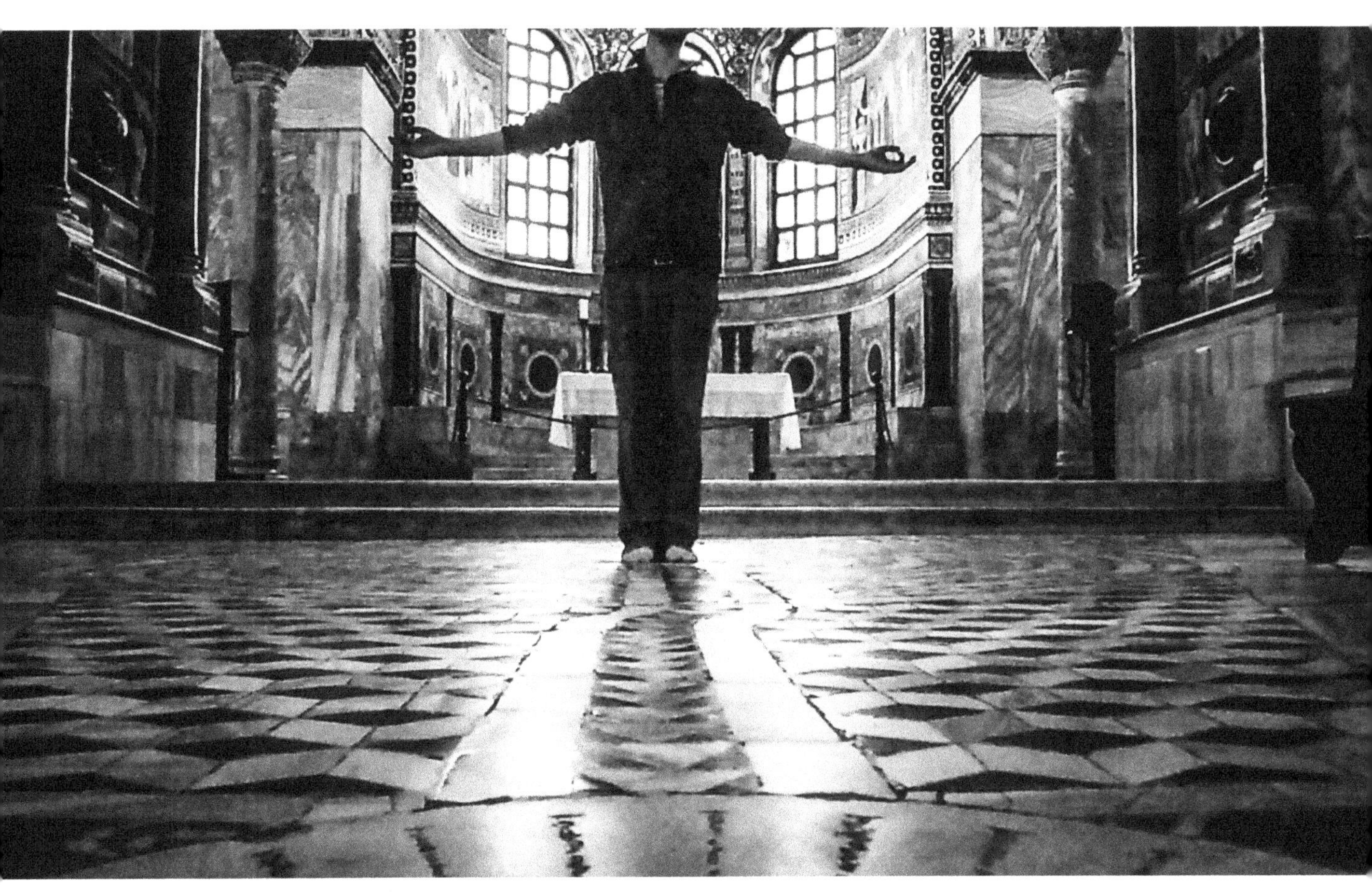

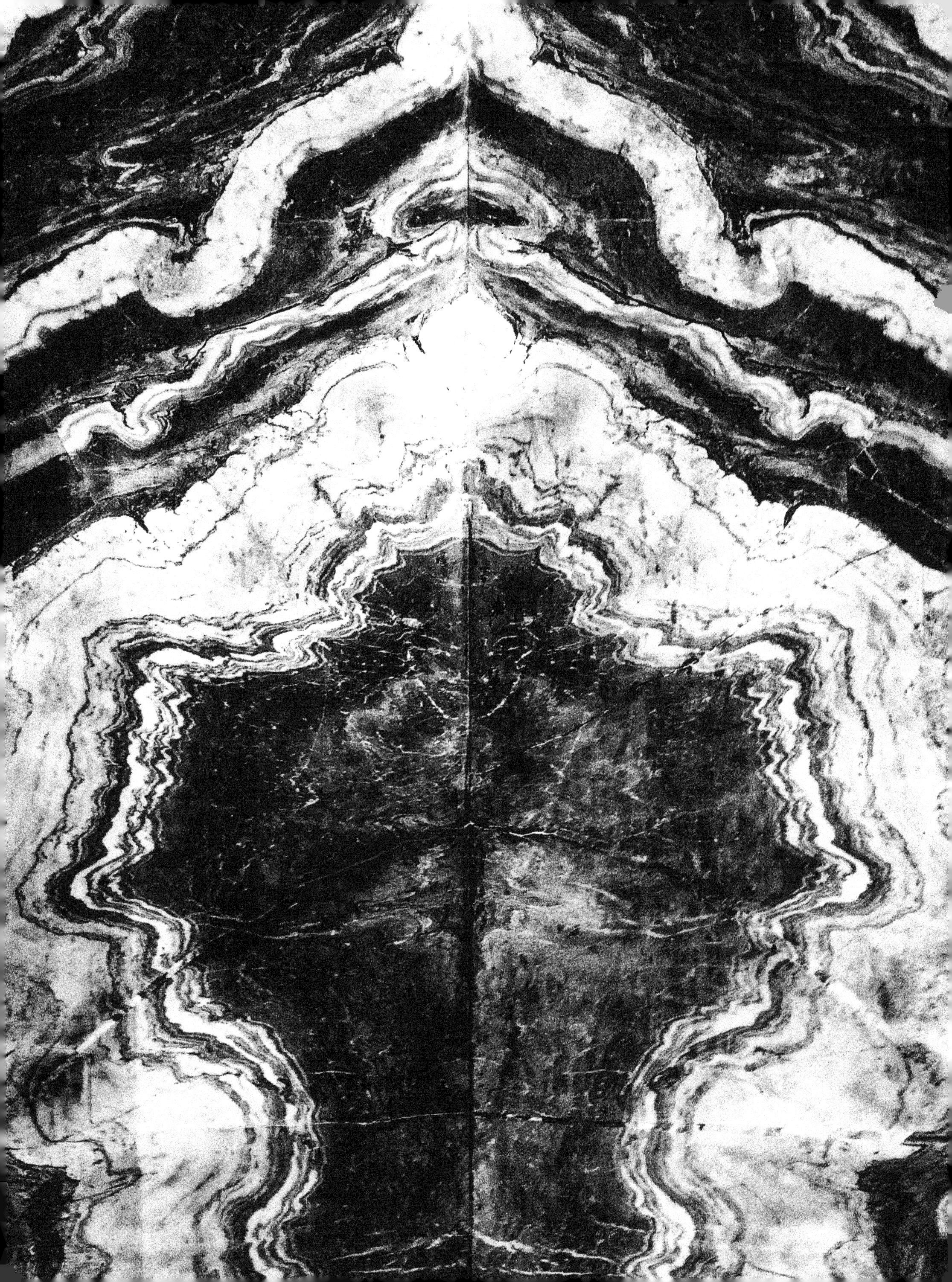

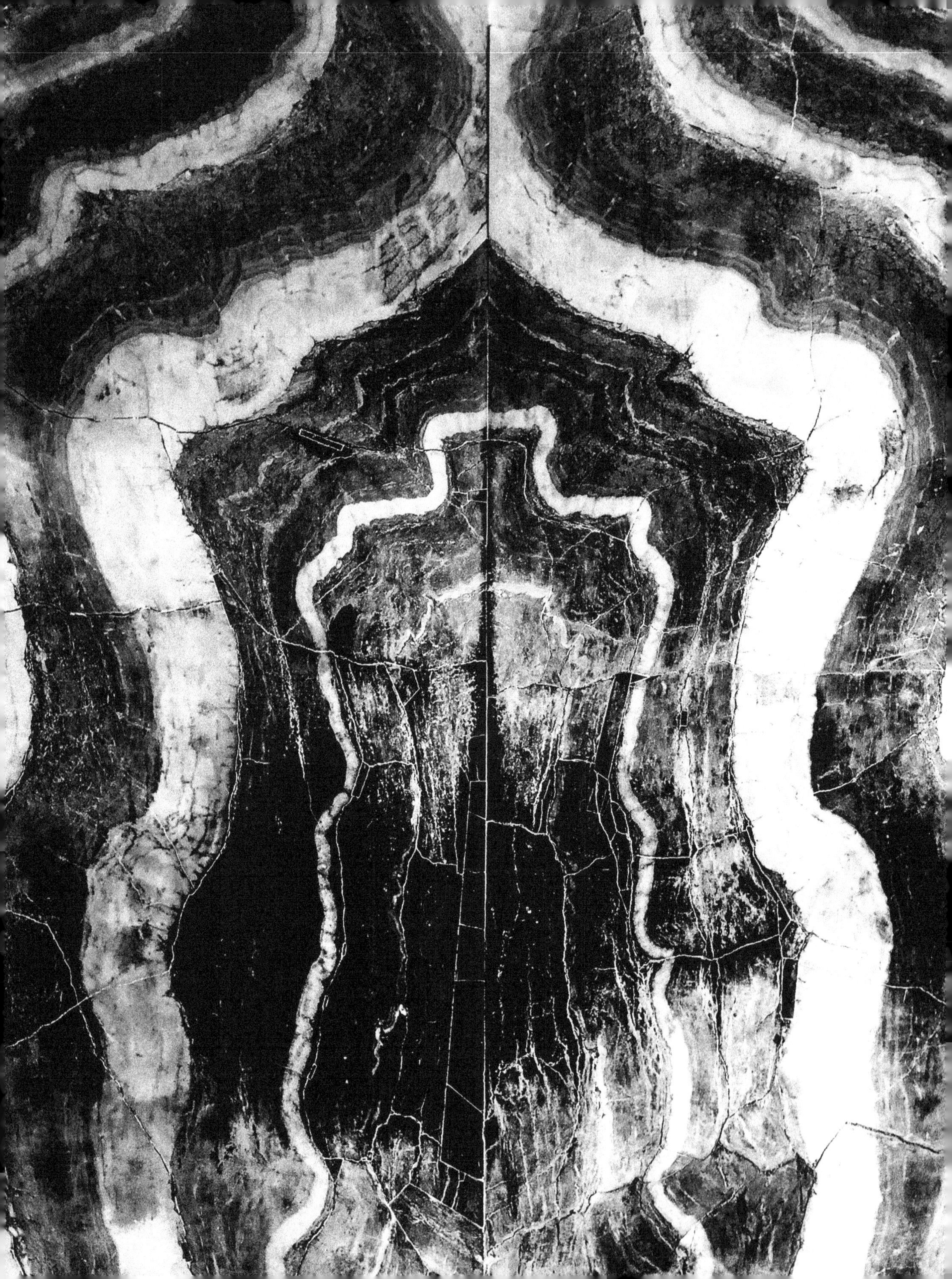

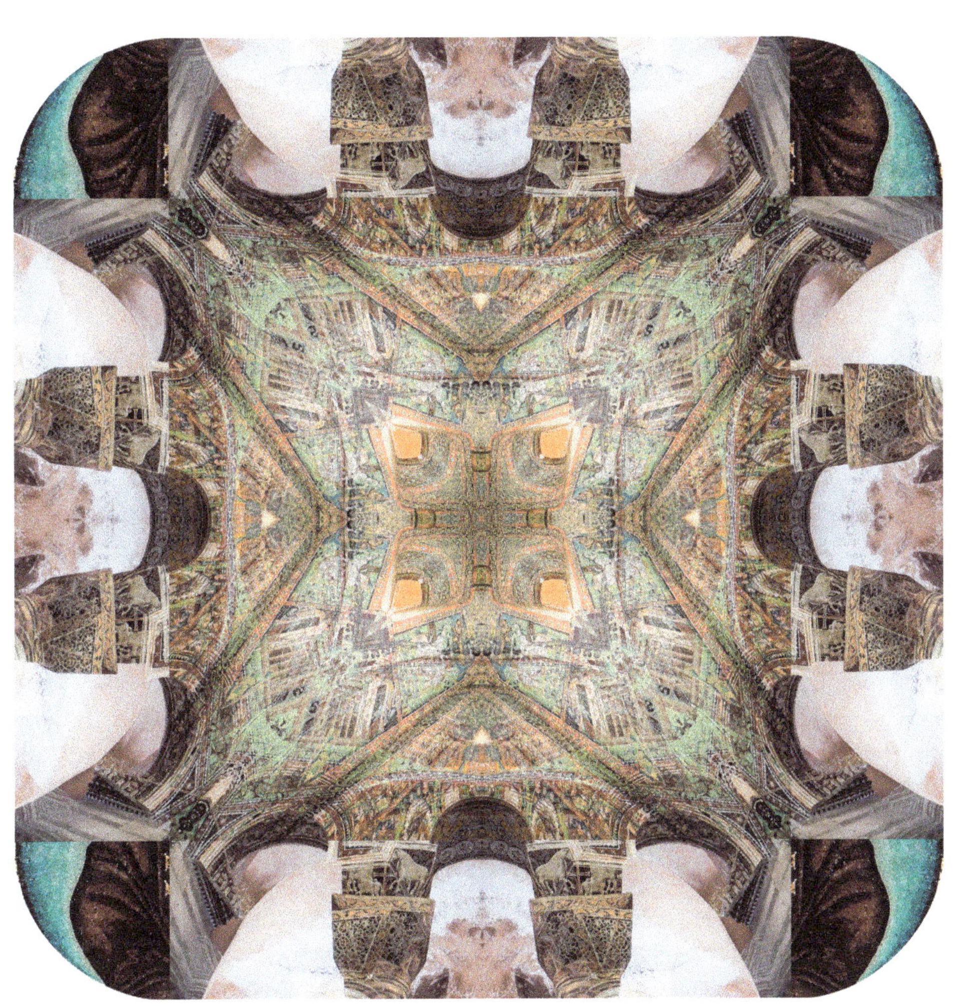

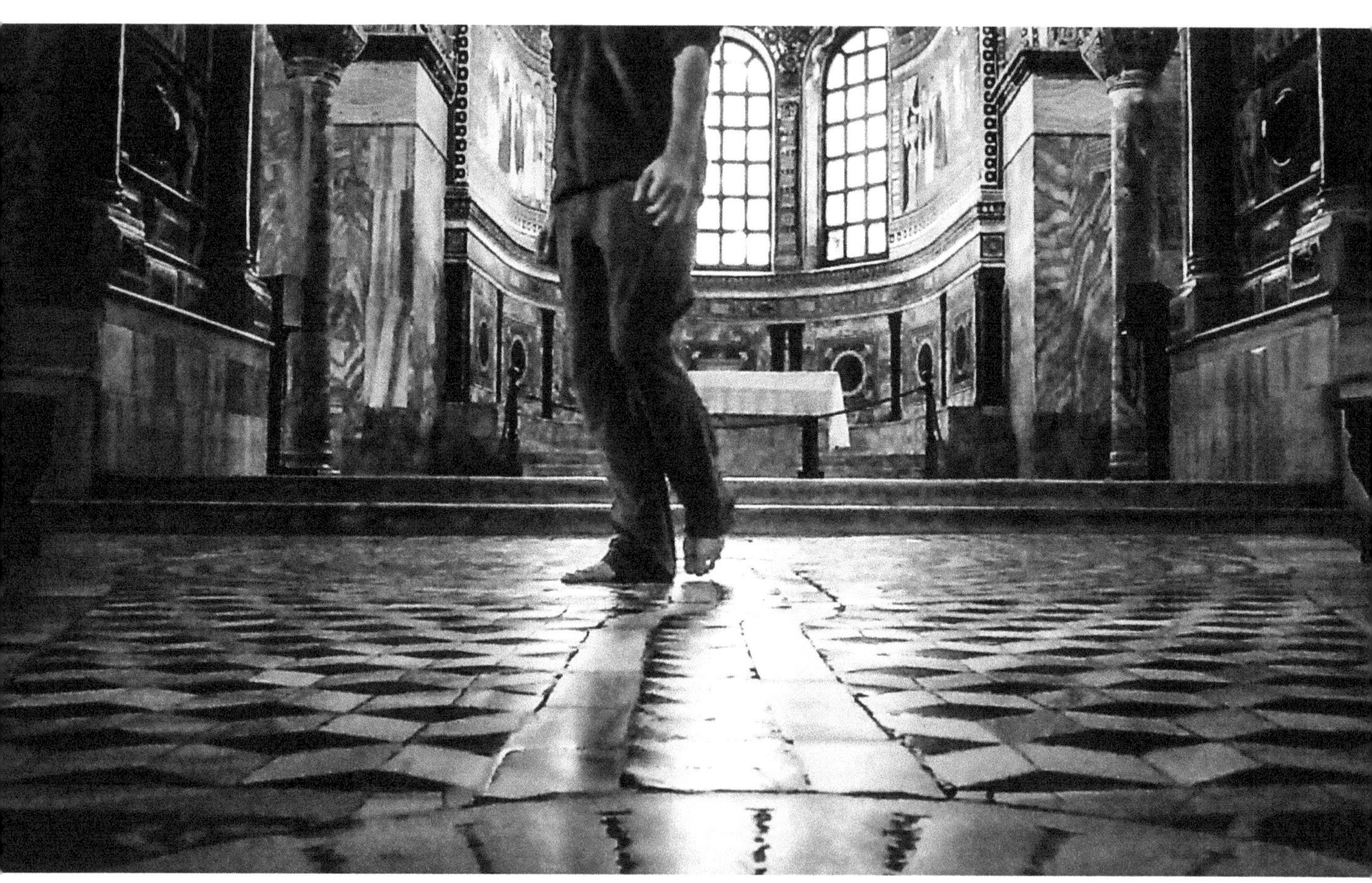

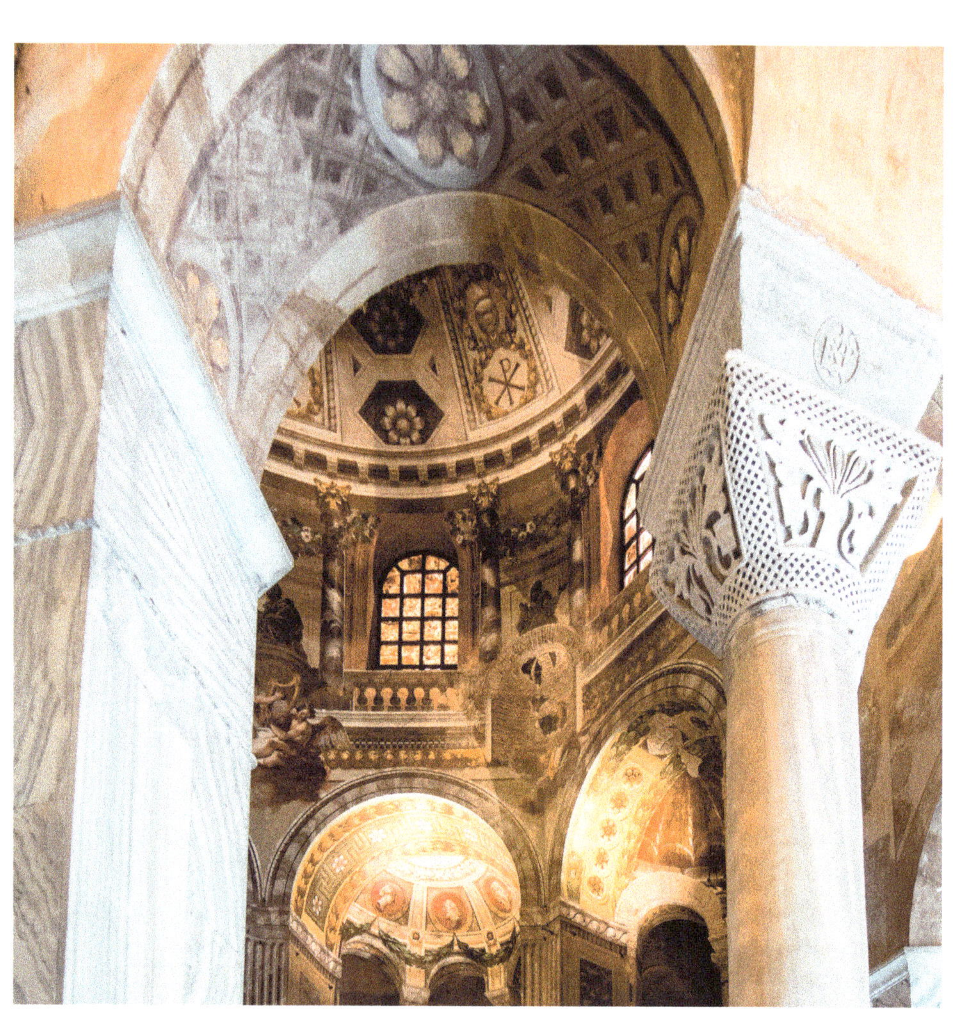

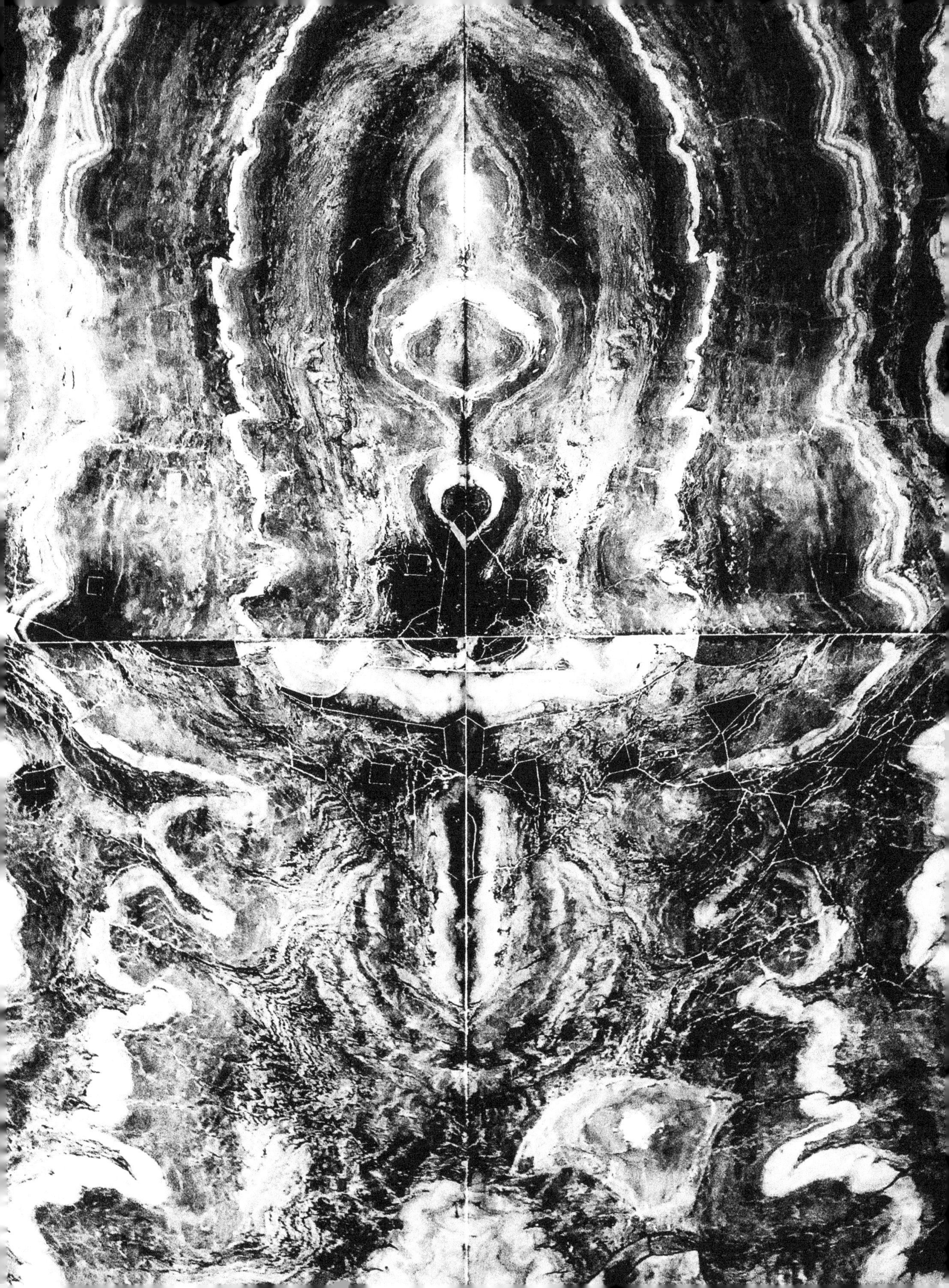

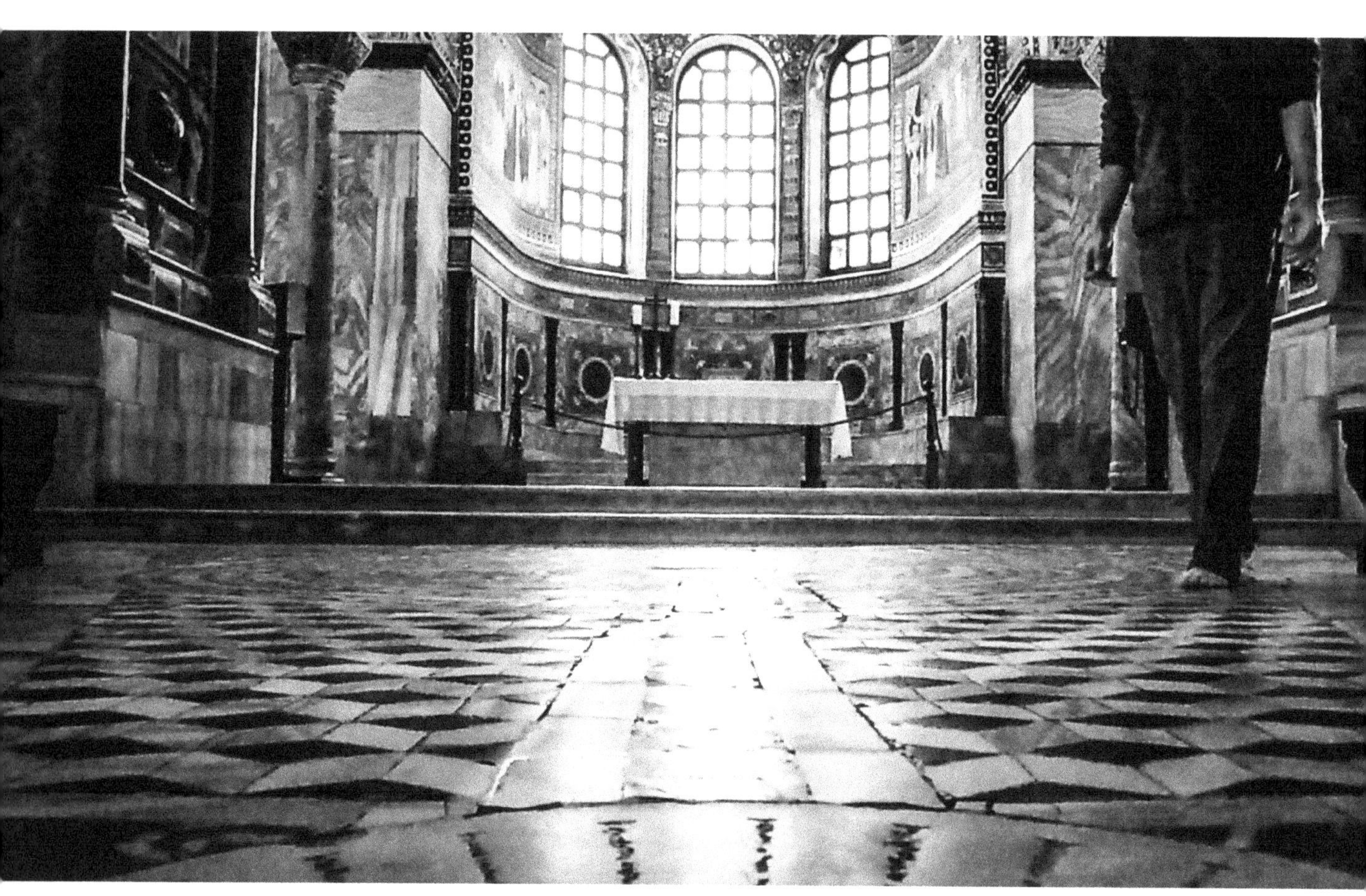

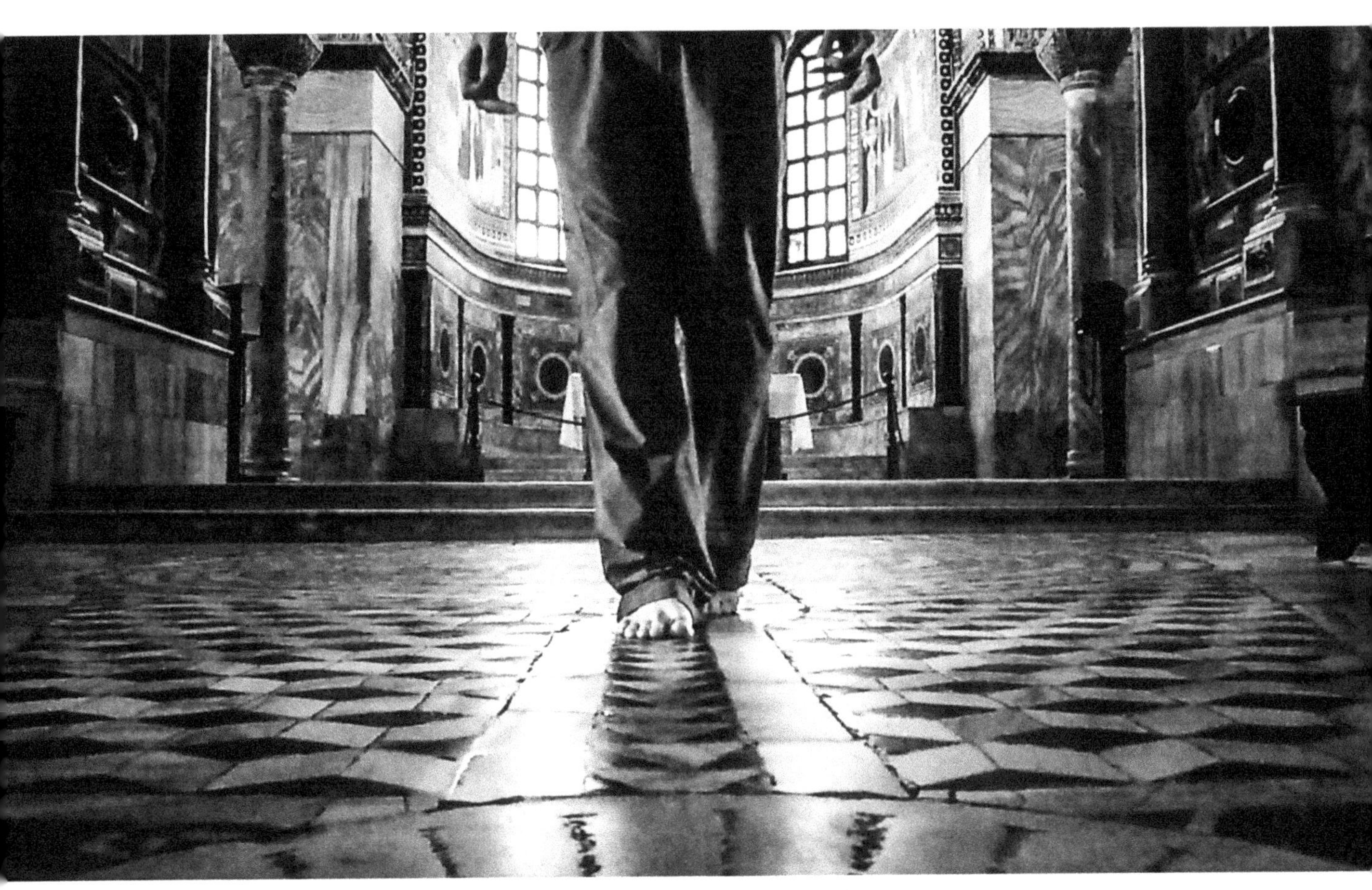

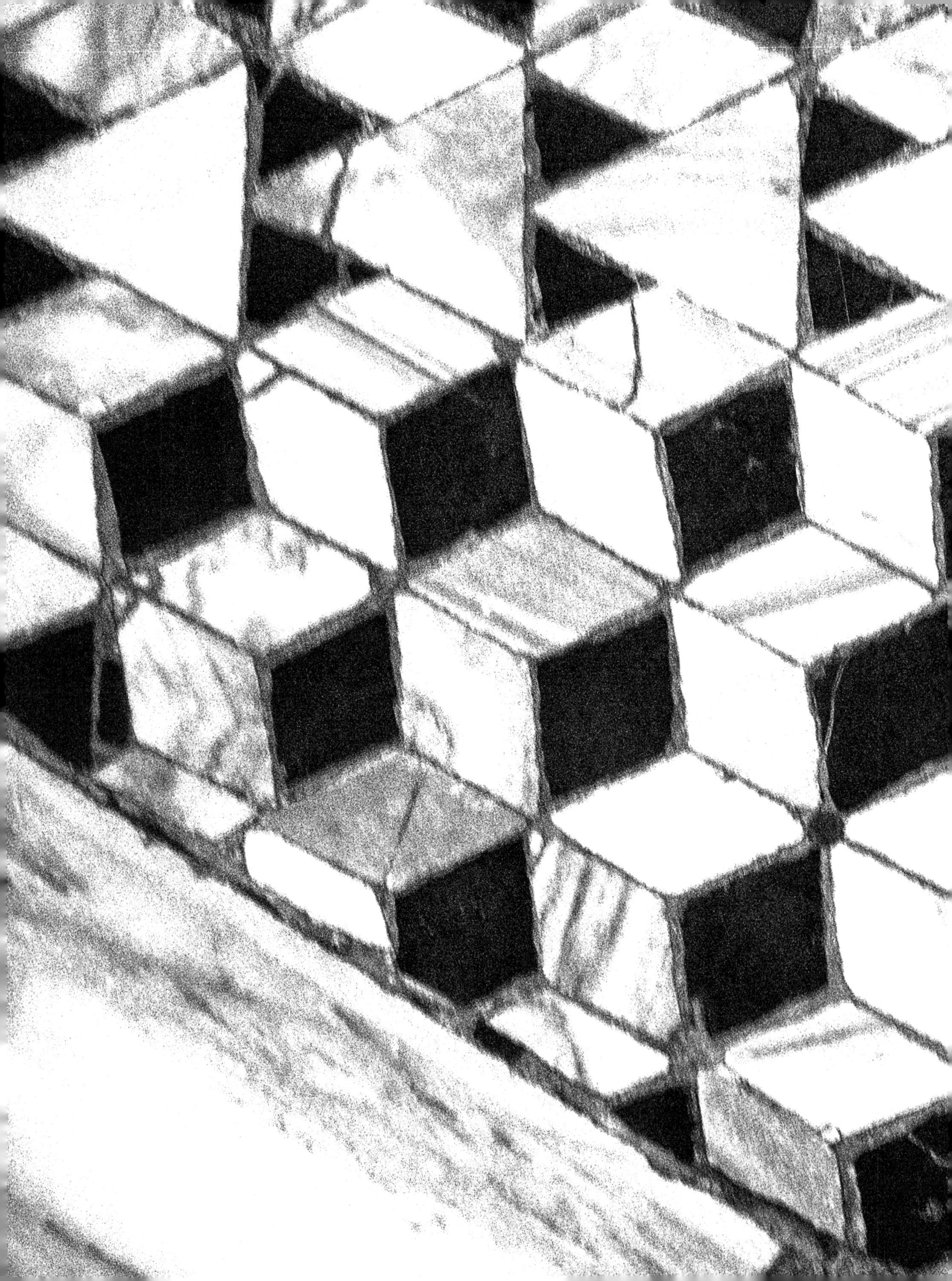

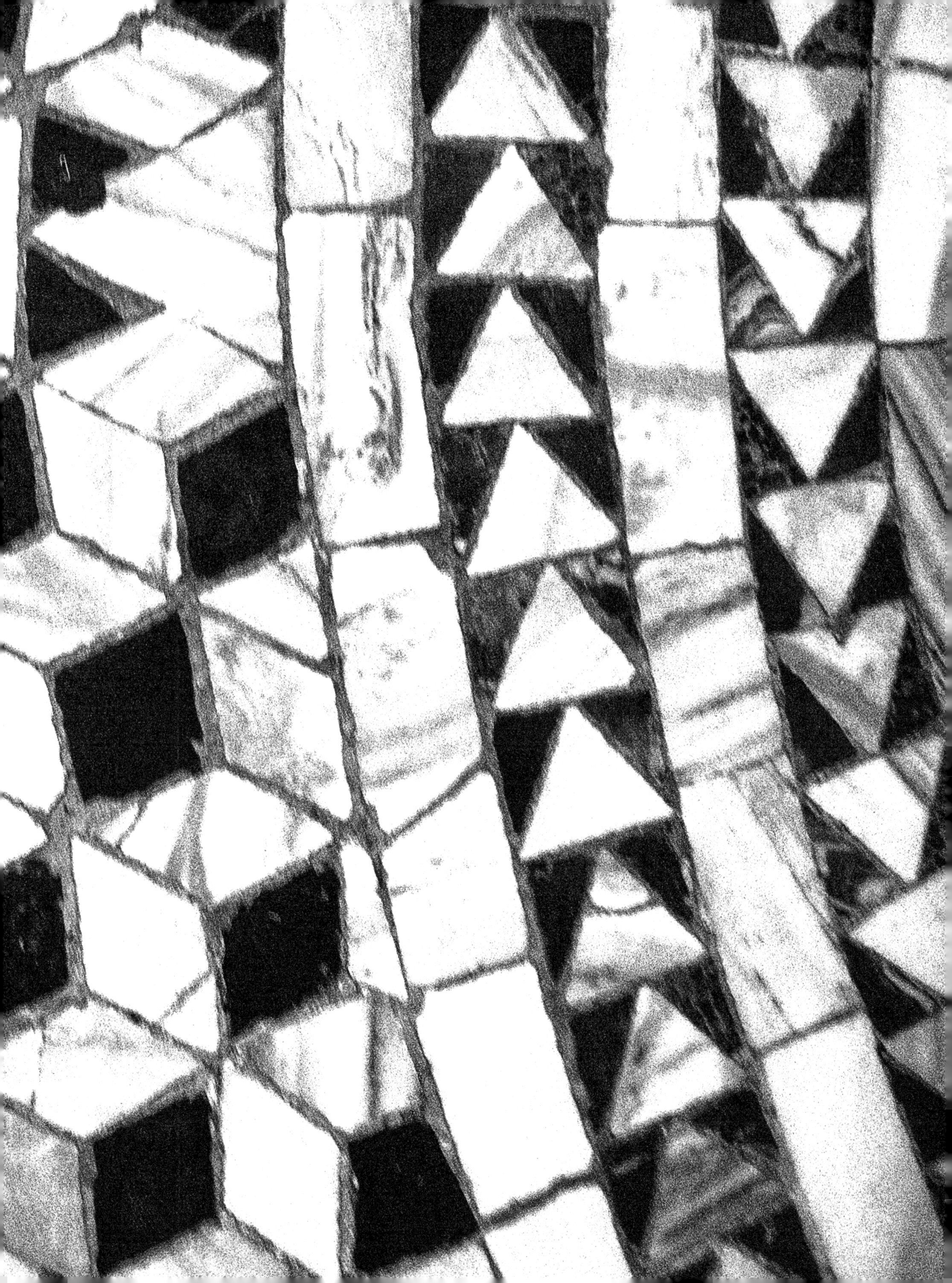

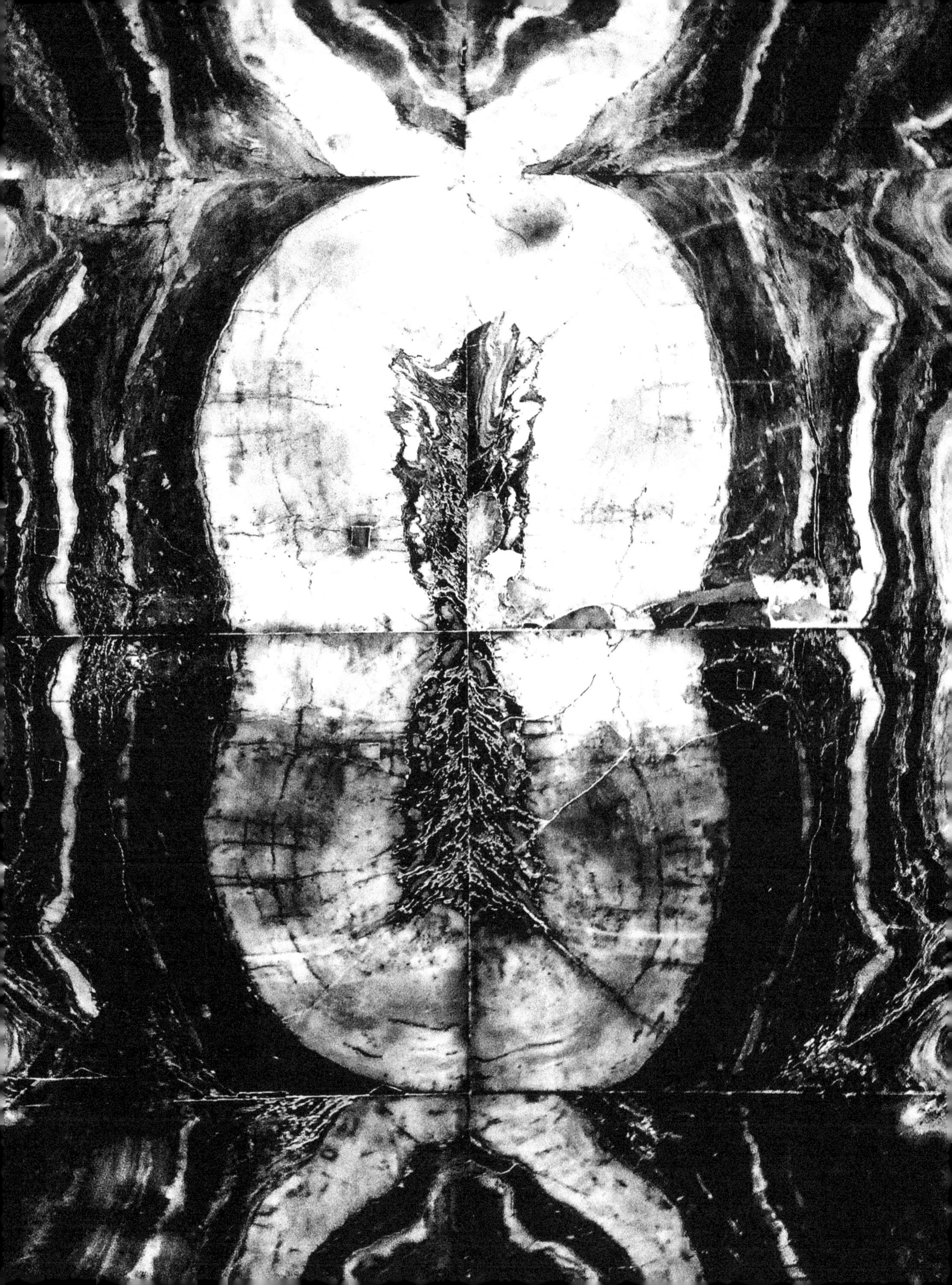

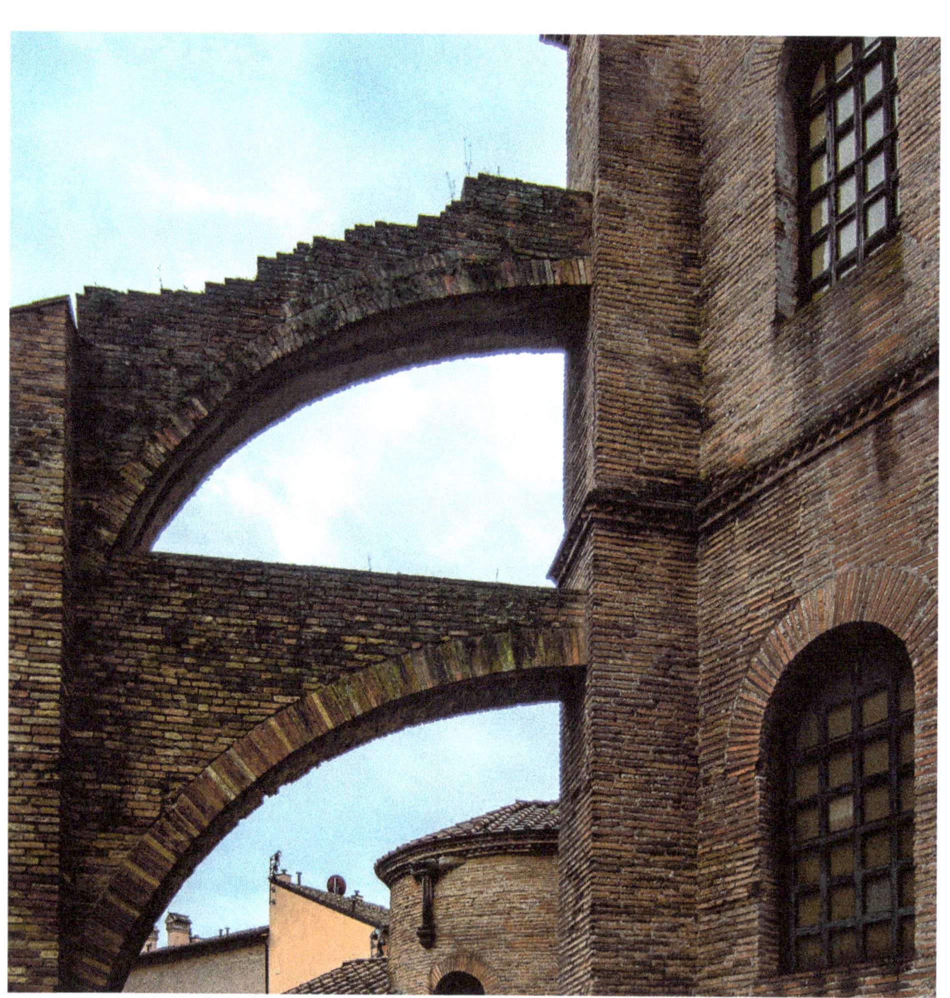

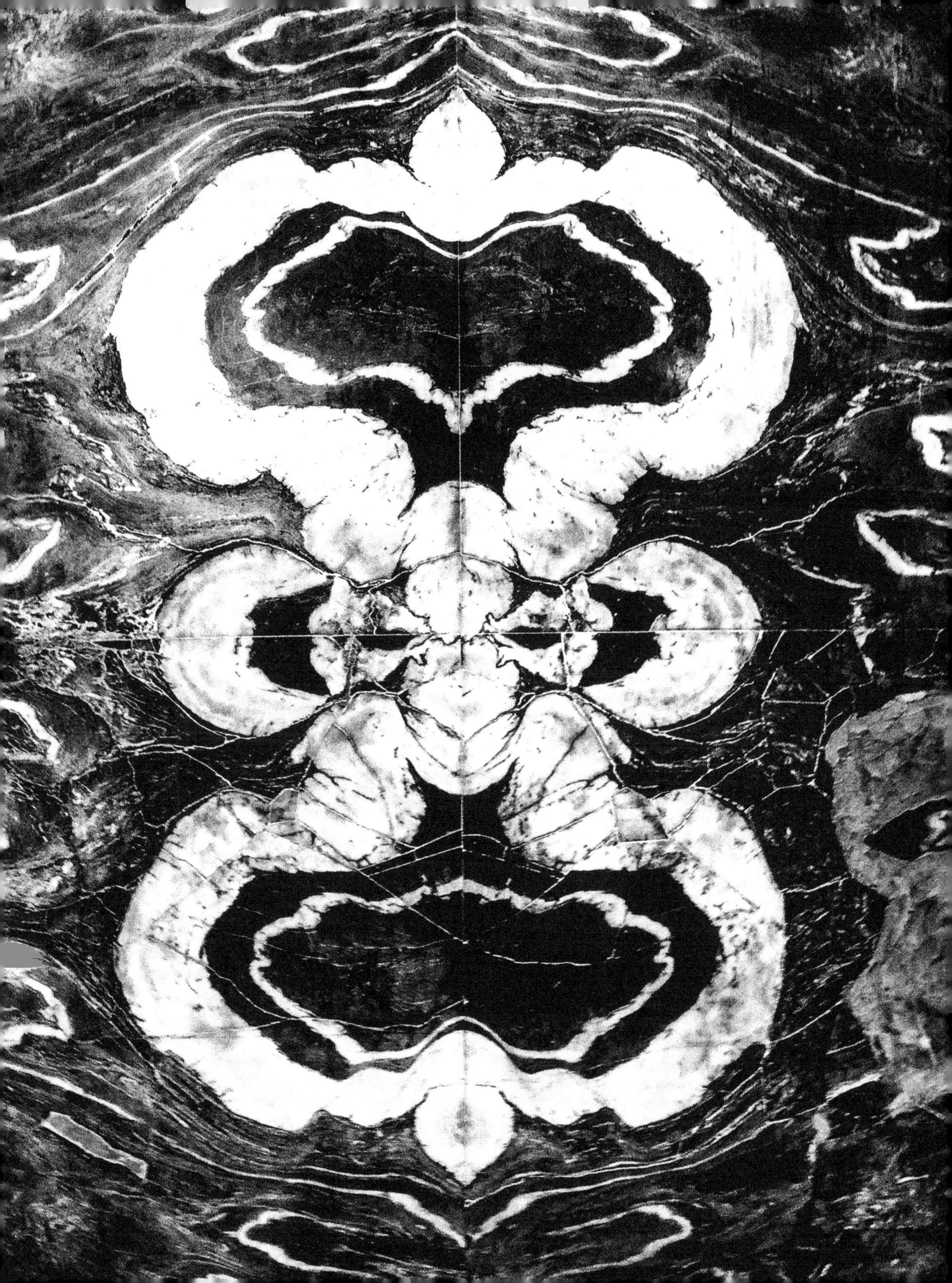

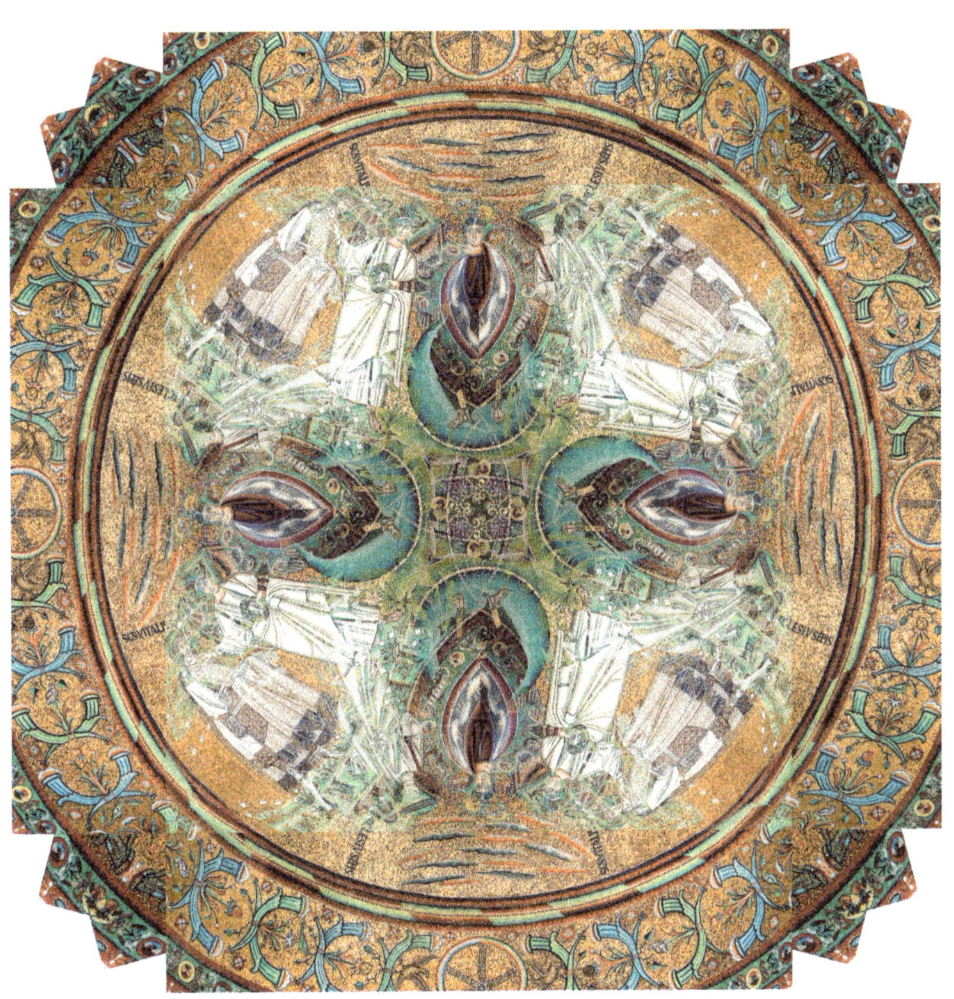

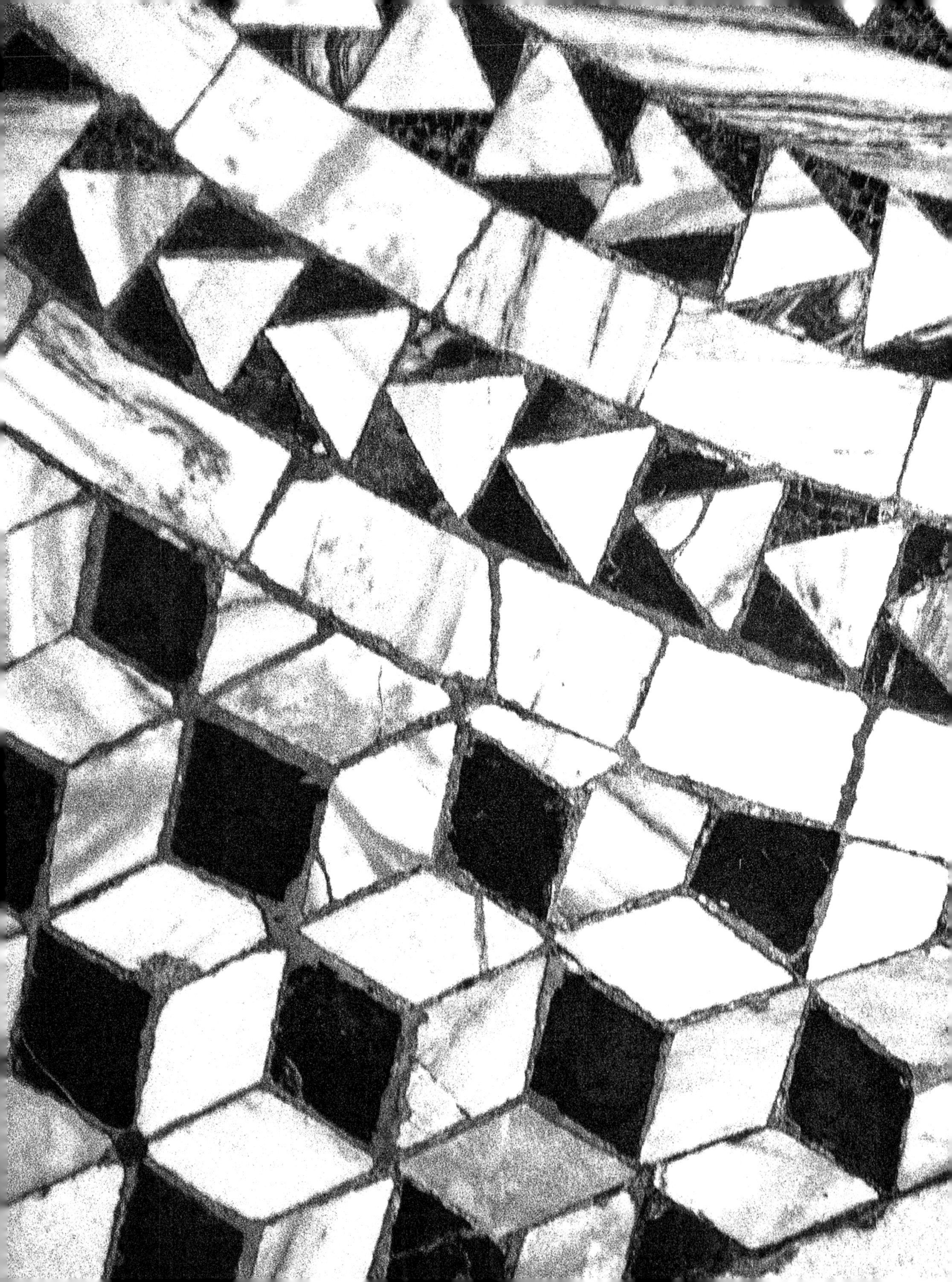

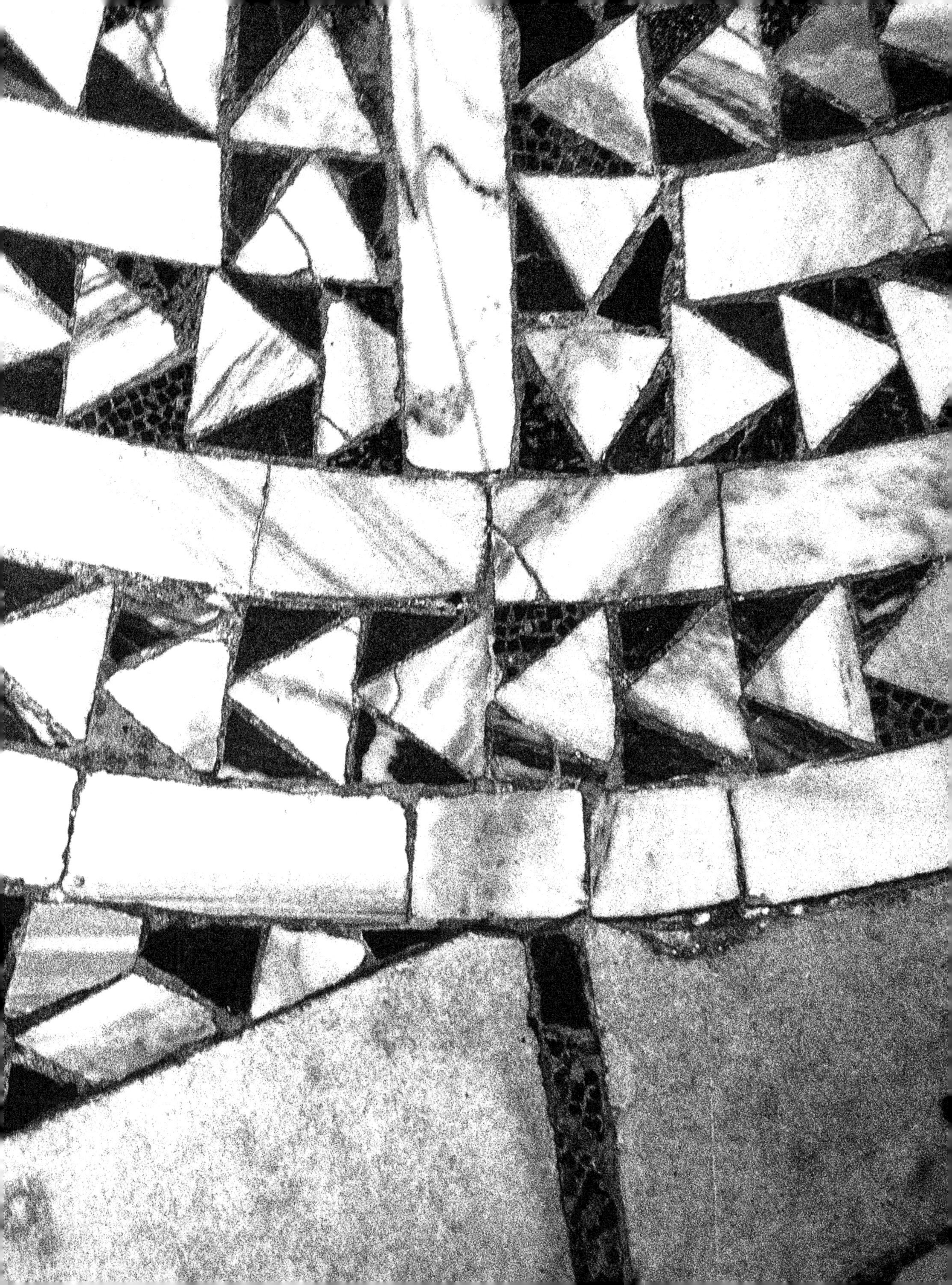

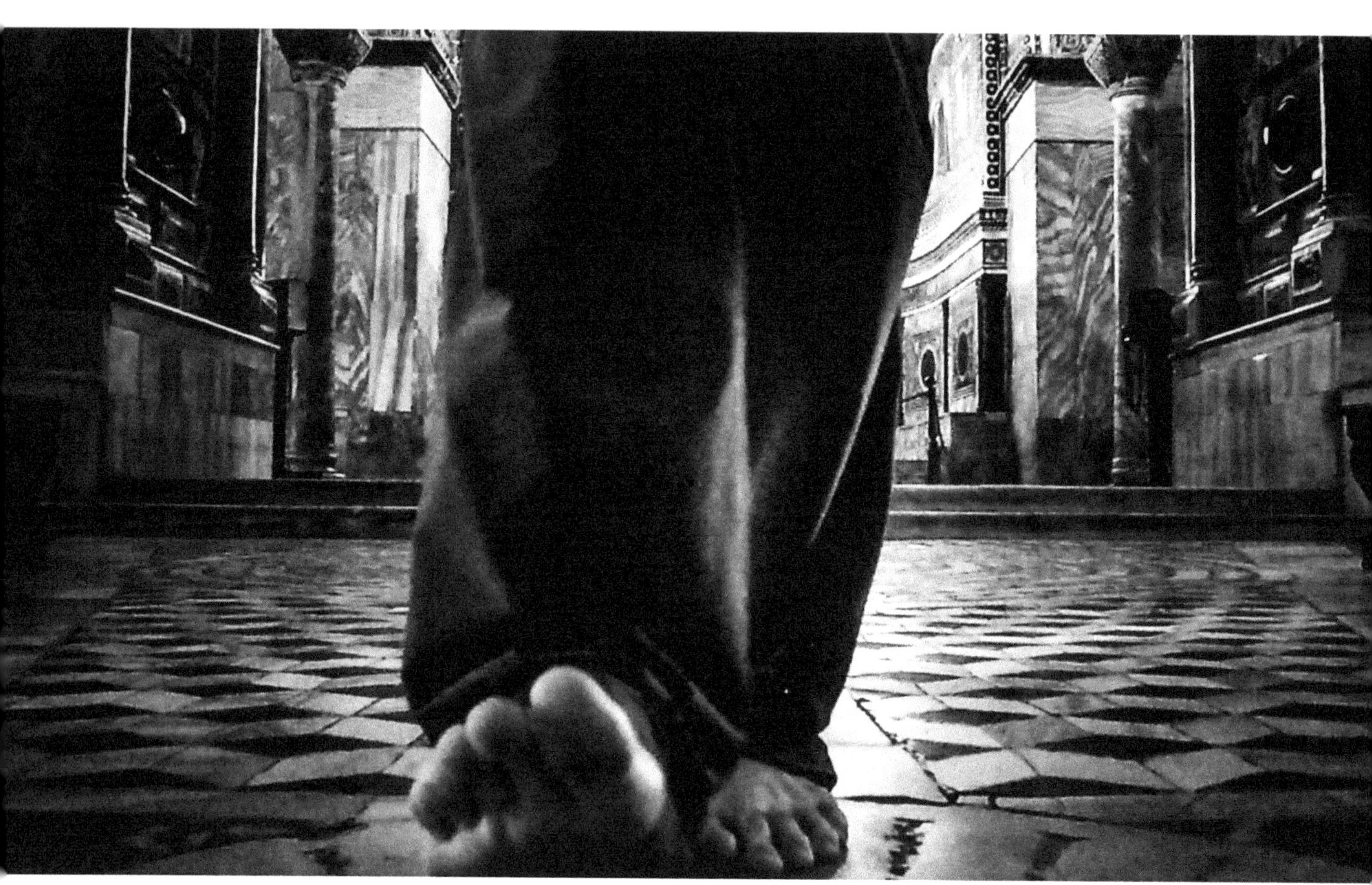

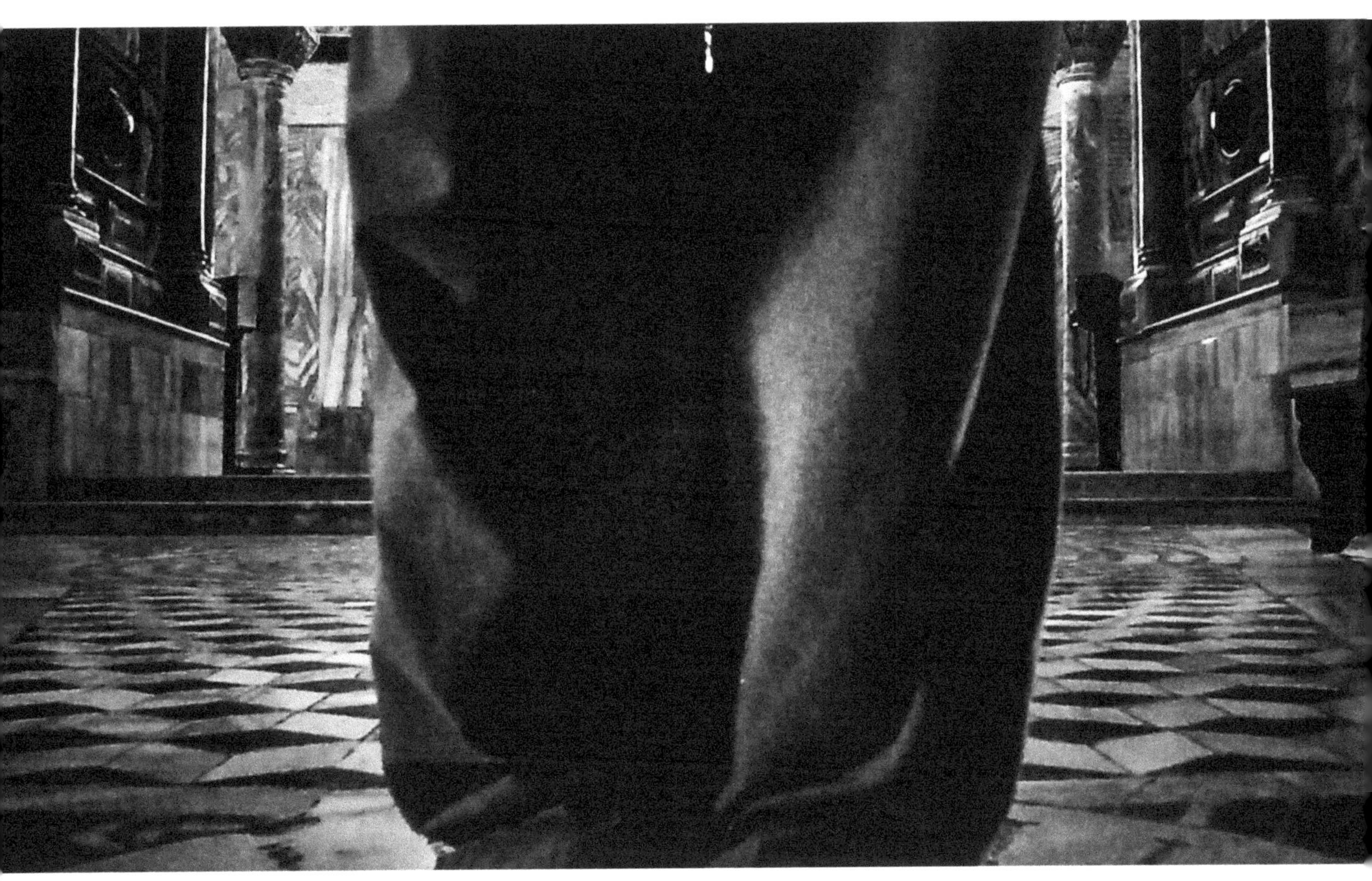

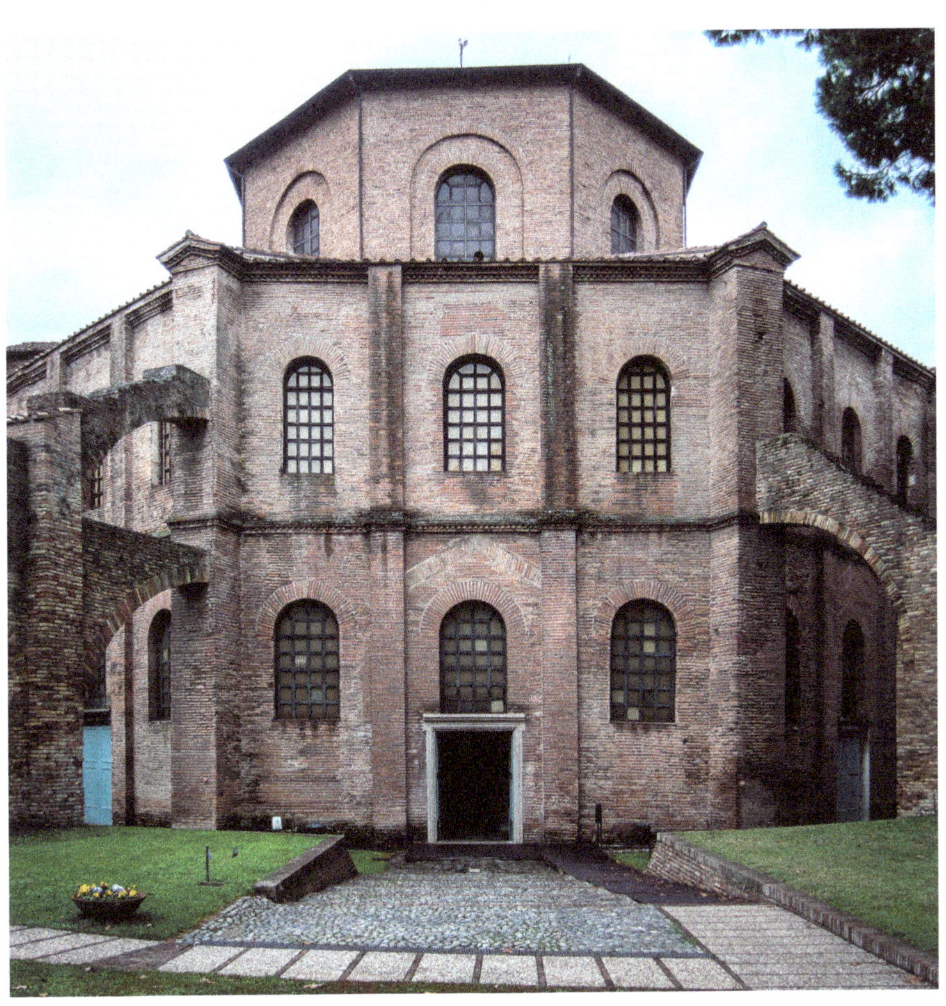

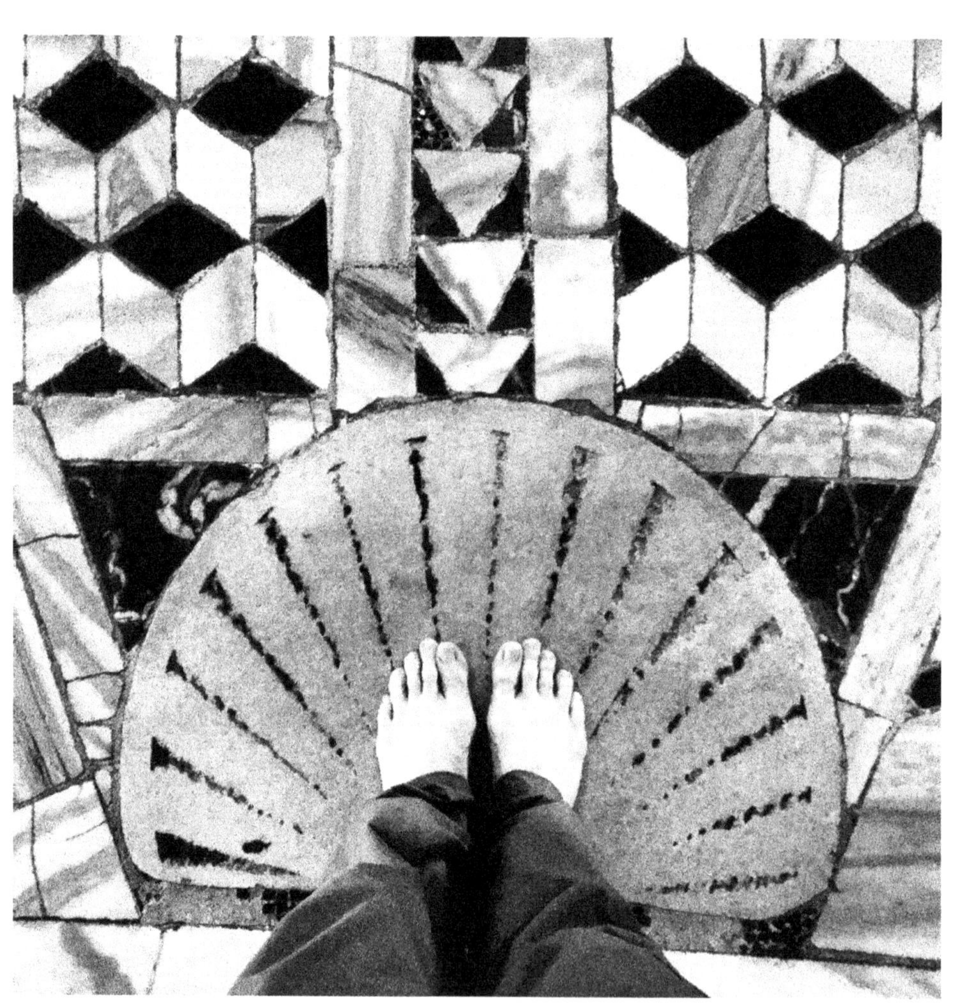

images

marble paintings, 2014, photographs

19, 24, 28, 31, 37, 38, 45, 49, 50, 61, 62, 67, 73, 75

labyrinth, 2014, video stills

23, 26, 27, 34, 40, 41, 53, 58, 59, 64, 68, 69, 80, 81

San Vitale, 2014, photographs

17, 18, 20/21, 25, 30, 32/33, 39, 42/43, 47, 48, 51, 54/55, 57, 66, 70/71, 74, 78/79, 83, 84

San Vitale, 2015, digital collage

36, 63, 77

Springtime in Byzantium

Published by bd-studios.com in New York City, 2021

Photography and Design by luke kurtis

"theodora" originally appeared in *the immeasurable fold*

ISBN 978-0-9992078-8-8

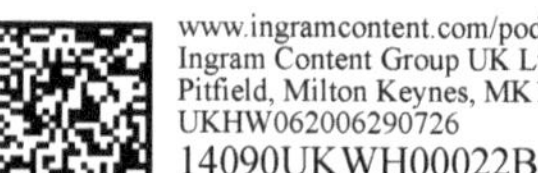

www.ingramcontent.com/pod-product-compliance
Ingram Content Group UK Ltd.
Pitfield, Milton Keynes, MK11 3LW, UK
UKHW062006290726
14090UKWH00022B/1424